THE FIRST 100 YEARS

Regular Edition:
ISBN 10: 1-56037-336-9
ISBN 13: 978-1-56037-336-0

Special Edition:
ISBN 10: 1-56037-479-9
ISBN 13: 978-1-56037-479-4

Editor: Jessica Solberg
Designer: Eric P. Hanson
Photo Librarian: Theresa Rush

Cover: Logan Pass. Photo by Tony Bynum.
Back flap: Tent camp. Courtesy Glacier National Park Archives.
Back cover: Tourists on Mount Stanton, with Sperry Glacier in background. T. J. Hileman.
Courtesy Glacier National Park Archives.
Map on page 4 by Dee Dee Dowden.

For more information on our books, write Farcountry Press, P.O. Box 5630, Helena, MT 59604;
call (800) 821-3874; or visit www.farcountrypress.com.

Library of Congress Cataloging-in-Publication Data

Guthrie, C. W.
  Glacier National Park : the first 100 years / by C.W. Guthrie.
    p. cm.
  ISBN-13: 978-1-56037-336-0
  ISBN-10: 1-56037-336-9
  1. Glacier National Park (Mont.)--History. I. Title.

  F737.G5G886 2008
  978.6'52--dc22

                        2007044650

Created, produced, and designed in the United States.
Printed in China.

13 12 11 10 09 08   1 2 3 4 5 6

Glacier National Park

THE FIRST 100 YEARS

By C. W. Guthrie

FARCOUNTRY
PRESS

HELENA, MONTANA

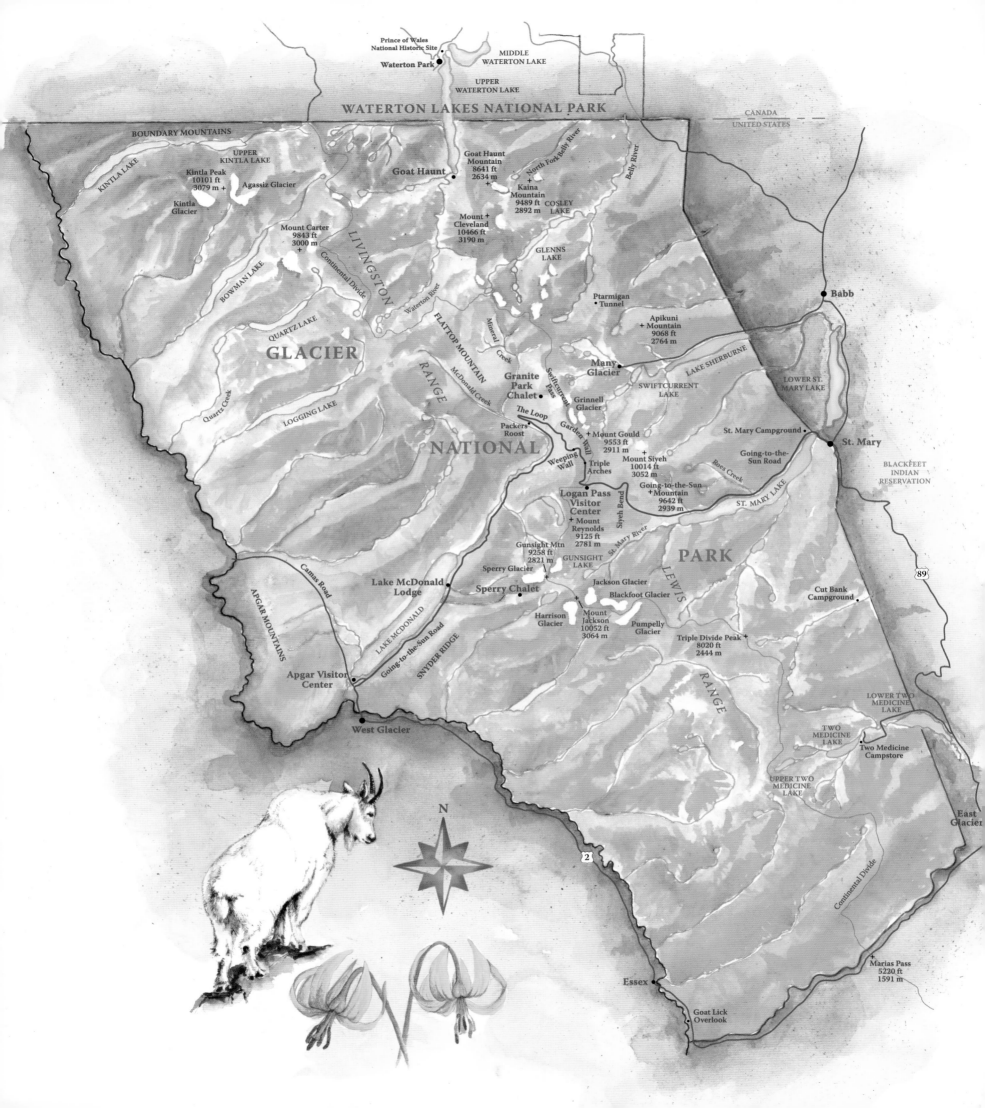

Prince of Wales
National Historic Site
Waterton Park

MIDDLE
WATERTON LAKE

UPPER
WATERTON LAKE

WATERTON LAKES NATIONAL PARK

CANADA
UNITED STATES

BOUNDARY MOUNTAINS

UPPER
KINTLA LAKE

Kintla Peak
10101 ft
3079 m +

KINTLA LAKE

Agassiz Glacier

Kintla
Glacier

Goat Haunt

Goat Haunt
Mountain
8641 ft
2634 m

North Fork Belly River

Belly River

+ Kaina
Mountain
9489 ft
2892 m

COSLEY
LAKE

Mount Carter
9843 ft
3000 m
+

LIVINGSTON

Continental Divide

+ Mount
Cleveland
10466 ft
3190 m

GLENNS
LAKE

Babb

BOWMAN LAKE

Waterton River

Ptarmigan
Tunnel

Apikuni
+ Mountain
9068 ft
2764 m

QUARTZ LAKE

GLACIER

FLATTOP MOUNTAIN

RANGE

Mineral Creek

McDonald Creek

**Many
Glacier**

LAKE SHERBURNE

SWIFTCURRENT
LAKE

LOWER ST.
MARY LAKE

**Granite
Park
Chalet**

Swiftcurrent Pass

Grinnell
Glacier

St. Mary Campground

St. Mary

Quartz Creek

LOGGING LAKE

The Loop

Packers
Roost

Garden Wall

+ Mount Gould
9553 ft
2911 m

Going-to-the-
Sun Road

BLACKFEET
INDIAN
RESERVATION

NATIONAL

Weeping
Wall

+ Triple
Arches

+ Mount Siyeh
10014 ft
3052 m

Roes Creek

Siyeh Bend

+ Going-to-the-Sun
Mountain
9642 ft
2939 m

ST. MARY LAKE

**Logan Pass
Visitor
Center**

+ Mount
Reynolds
9125 ft
2781 m

St. Mary River

PARK

Gunsight Mtn
9258 ft
2821 m

Sperry Glacier

GUNSIGHT
LAKE

Camas Road

**Lake McDonald
Lodge**

Jackson Glacier

Sperry Chalet

Blackfoot Glacier

LEWIS

Cut Bank
Campground

89

APGAR MOUNTAINS

Harrison
Glacier

Mount
Jackson
10052 ft
3064 m

Pumpelly
Glacier

LAKE MCDONALD

Going-to-the-Sun Road

SNYDER RIDGE

Triple Divide Peak +
8020 ft
2444 m

RANGE

**Apgar Visitor
Center**

LOWER TWO
MEDICINE
LAKE

N

TWO
MEDICINE
LAKE

West Glacier

Two Medicine
Campstore

UPPER TWO
MEDICINE
LAKE

East
Glacier

2

Continental Divide

Essex

Marias Pass
5220 ft
1591 m

Goat Lick
Overlook

Contents

Avalanche Creek Gorge.
Photo by John Reddy.

Foreword

by Deirdre Shaw, Museum Curator, Glacier National Park

FOR THOUSANDS OF YEARS, people have been drawn to the rich landscape now defined as Glacier National Park. Seeking sustenance, refuge, adventure, and knowledge, people have reveled in the region's dramatic physical features and the diversity of flora and fauna. The Blackfeet, Salish, Kootenai, Assiniboine, and other tribes have a relationship with this land that goes back thousands of years. The ecosystem provided the tribes not only with food and shelter, it informed their rich culture and spiritual traditions. Their connection with the landscape continues today.

The settlement of the American West prompted an increased government presence and the further development of federal land management philosophies and policies. By the late 1890s, cartographic demarcations drawn across this once open landscape firmly delineated national, state, and tribal boundaries and jurisdictions. The perceived end of the western frontier triggered a concern among some Americans that the wildness of places like Glacier would soon be gone. The resulting movement sparked the creation of national parks and other conservation agencies, which seek to preserve a bit of the pristine frontier for future generations.

Mount Reynolds.
Photo by Tony Bynum.

In 1910, Glacier National Park was established, preserving 1 million acres of northwestern Montana for the American public to enjoy. In the park's legislation, the U.S. Congress stated that Glacier would be "a public pleasuring ground" preserved in "a state of nature."

Since the park was established, park managers, park concessionaires, and private landowners have helped shape Glacier National Park into one of the country's most beloved national parks.

From the landmark construction of the Going-to-the-Sun Road to George Bird Grinnell, C. M. Russell, and other famed writers and artists who have captured Glacier's beauty in words and images, the story of Glacier National Park is a colorful and inspiring one.

Glacier has long beckoned visitors to its unmatched landscape, and it continues to do so today, as we celebrate the park's first 100 years. Today's park visitors seek much the same experience as those explorers of the past: spiritual sustenance, respite, wilderness adventure, knowledge, and just plain fun. Understanding the history of this special place will only enhance one's experience.

A tour boat on Swiftcurrent Lake cruises past Grinnell Point.
Photo by John Reddy.

Acknowledgments

My deep appreciation to the amazing people I have been so privileged to work with on this project. I am sincerely grateful to Ann Fagre and Deirdre Shaw of the Glacier National Park Archives. These accomplished women are a researcher's dream; they are delightful to work with and they know Glacier. A special thanks to Ann for her extraordinary effort in providing many of the photographs in this book. She worked tirelessly, digging through volumes of photographs and documents, and was greatly patient with me while I pondered and asked for even more photographs.

Westside waterfalls during spring runoff.
Photo by John Reddy.

I wish to also thank Patsi Morton, daughter of Mel Ruder, for graciously allowing me to use her father's photographs. He spent many years photographing Glacier National Park and left a grand legacy.

Much is also owed John Chase of Great Falls for his help and the use of his remarkable collection of historic documents and photographs. John is part of one of Glacier's famed family dynasties. Trapper Tom Dawson's daughter Lorena Clarke Dawson married Will Meade, and their daughter Isabel married John's Uncle Ralph Chase. Ralph and John's father Myron worked at Glacier for many years. John has been providing displays of park history every summer at the Glacier Park Lodge in East Glacier since the late 1990s. These popular displays provide visitors a window into Glacier's past.

There are not adequate words to express how much I appreciate the help and guidance of Dr. Dan Fagre, ecologist for the USGS Northern Rocky Mountain Science Center; Jack Potter, Glacier National Park Sciences and Resource Management; Lon Johnson, Cultural Resources; and John Waller, wildlife biologist. Thank you.

Thanks also to Don Loeffler, a prolific writer who has provided a wealth of information about his personal experiences as a mountaineer. He was a summer employee in Glacier National Park in the 1940s and is one of the thousands who return to Glacier often, reminding us that this park is truly unforgettable.

Thanks to Dr. Brian Reeves and the Blackfeet elders for their insights provided in the National Park Service study "Our Mountains are our Pillows." Thanks are also due Wendy Hill and Stephan Prince of the Glacier Natural History Association for their always cheerful support.

I take one last moment to honor the memory of two great ladies: Jean Liebig Soldowski and Frances Liebig, the daughters of Glacier's first forest ranger, Frank Liebig. Their lives began in Glacier, and their ninety-plus years were lived well and honorably spent as country schoolteachers in Montana.

The Going-to-the-Sun Road winds through
a forest of gold in autumn.
©chuckhaney.com.

Introduction

More than a Place

"I WOULDN'T TRADE *one square mile of Glacier for all the other parks put together. The vast valleys that you look down into, and the unbelievably great peaks and ridges rising above you, and the hidden passes and the surprising banks of snow, and the incongruous meadows on the high flats, and the tumbling white streams, and the flowers and the silent little lakes around a bend— all have an isolation and a calm majesty that to me make Glacier Park more than just a place," wrote famed author and war correspondent Ernie Pyle in a 1935 story in* Home Country. *Those who have experienced the magnificence of these mountains and valleys will agree. Glacier National Park is more than a place. It is majesty.*

In 2010 these majestic million-plus acres celebrate 100 years as a national park. Together with Waterton Lakes National Park, Glacier also celebrates seventy-eight years as an International Peace Park, thirty-one years as the world's first joining biosphere reserves, and fifteen years as a World Heritage Site. *These designations acknowledge the two parks' importance to the nation and to the world.*

The history of Glacier is full of events and characters, ranging from the ancient upheavals that created the land formations and the artistic whittling of glaciers, to the Native American tribes that first occupied its mountains and valleys, to the coming of the fur trappers, explorers, and settlers, to the land's preservation as a national park. As a park its history is one of development as a tourist destination with Swiss-style hotels and chalets and the remarkable Going-to-the-Sun Road; protection of wildlife; and worldwide recognition as an International Peace Park, World Biosphere Reserve, and World Heritage Site.

This book is a brief and lively tour through that history to commemorate Glacier's 100th anniversary as a national park. Alas, there is so much more story than can be told in these pages. Please forgive my sins of omission.

Three Monarchs, *Mark Ogle.*
Courtesy Mark Ogle Studios, Kalispell, Montana.

I. Crown of the Continent

Beargrass adorns the mountainsides above Grinnell Lake.

©chuckhaney.com

The Crown of the Continent Takes Shape

POWERFUL FORCES OF NATURE *formed the spectacular jagged peaks, alpine panoramas, flowered meadows, deep mountain lakes, sparkling rivers, and great wooded valleys that are Glacier National Park. Known as the Crown of the Continent, a phrase coined by explorer and geologist George Bird Grinnell in 1901, Glacier National Park encompasses soaring peaks that form part of the long spine of the Continental Divide within the Rocky Mountains. Yet Glacier's mountains stand alone in raw, magnificent grandeur. Their incredible story began more than a billion years ago.*

The Making of the Mountains

The stunning concentration of peerless peaks and valleys we now call Glacier National Park had humble beginnings. Approximately 1.5 billion years ago, they were the floor of a shallow sea-filled trough that extended from the Arctic Ocean through western North America to Mexico. Runoff from nearby barren hills and waves lapping the shore deposited sediment onto the sea floor. Over millions of years the sediment hardened into thick layers of limestone, mudstone, and sandstone—the start of a period of slow mountain making.

About 170 million years ago, while dinosaurs still roamed the earth, the mountain making sped up. On the western edge of the North American continent, the earth's tectonic plates violently collided, forcing the land to wrinkle and uplift and forming the ancestral Rocky Mountains.

Millions of years of additional stresses followed. Tremendous forces squeezed a massive chunk of rock into a great fold, upturning the billion-year-old limestone, mudstone, and sandstone from the ancient seabed and breaking the earth's crust. Over millions of years this massive fold of rock was pushed fifty miles eastward and thrust over newer, softer rock formed a mere 60 to 70 million years ago. This great overthrust of earth, known as the Lewis Overthrust Fault, created Glacier's Lewis and Livingston mountain ranges.

Most mountain ranges feature uplifted older rock beneath younger rock. The mountains of Glacier defy the natural order; billion-year-old rock is perched on top of 60- to 70-million-year-old rock. On many of Glacier's ridges and slopes, you can see evidence of fossilized algae and other features of sedimentation— reminders that those high mountains were once the bottom of an ancient sea.

The Glaciers' Artistry

Spectacular geological events created the raw materials for the area's unique landscape, but it was glaciers that sculpted the masterpiece that is now Glacier National Park.

Chief Mountain is the best example of the Lewis Overthrust Fault, in which ancient rock lies on top of much younger rock.
©chuckhaney.com.

A glacier is a slow-moving mass of ice formed by the accumulation and compaction of snow. As snow accumulates year after year without melting, the weight of the snow presses down and compacts into layers of ice. The lower layers of ice are flexible, allowing the glacier to move downhill by the force of gravity.

During the last ice age—20,000 to 11,000 years ago—a sheet of ice thousands of feet thick covered a third of the continent and all but the highest peaks in what is now Glacier National Park. When the ice age ended and the earth warmed, gravity slowly pulled the melting glacial ice downward. As the glaciers worked their way around and down the mountains, they picked up ice, gravel, and rock debris. This sawtooth mixture carved the raw landscape into the magnificent peaks we see today. (Melting glaciers from the three previous ice ages in the last 2 million years may have had a hand in sculpting the mountains, too, but geologists credit the last ice age as the primary sculptor.)

The glaciers' grand works include a variety of unique formations: arêtes, horns, cirques, hanging valleys, U-shaped valleys, and moraines. Arêtes (*uh-RATES*) formed when two glaciers on opposite sides of a rock wall gnawed toward each other, creating a narrow, knife-edge ridge. The Garden Wall and the Ptarmigan and Pinnacle walls are excellent examples.

A horn, such as those found on Fusillade Mountain, Mount Reynolds, the Little Matterhorn, and Kinnerly Peak, formed when several glaciers whittled on all sides of a mountain to sculpt a prominent vertical peak.

Glaciers also scoured out bowls, which later filled with water, forming cirques (*serks*) such as Avalanche, Iceberg, and Gunsight lakes.

When smaller glaciers flowed into larger glaciers, their glacial tracks did not cut as deep. Their scant efforts left small valleys hanging on the mountainsides above larger valleys. These hanging valleys are most evident where waterfalls cascade over the lip of a valley; at Mount Oberlin, Bird Woman Falls plunges from a hanging valley thousands of feet into McDonald Valley, and Virginia Falls drops over a hanging

Although today's glaciers are not the massive ice age glaciers that shaped Glacier National Park, some of the glacial ice may have survived the warming period after the last ice age, making these glaciers at least 7,000 years old.
©chuckhaney.com.

valley between Little Chief and Dusty Star mountains into St. Mary Valley.

The glaciers then joined forces and gouged the impressive U-shaped valleys of St. Mary and McDonald and went on to scour the valleys of Two Medicine, Swiftcurrent, and Red Eagle.

When the glaciers were done, they left a residue of moraines—masses of rock and dirt debris—to mark

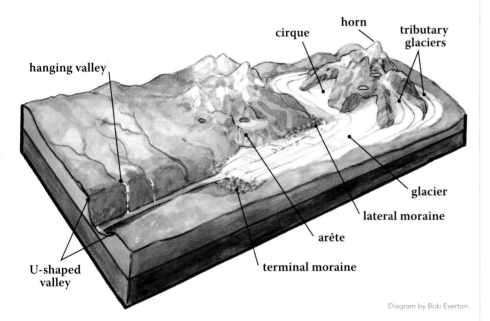

Diagram by Bob Everton.

where they came from, the path they took, and the place they finally melted into the earth.

The sculpting of the mountains and valleys continues today. They are changing in nearly imperceptible ways: by the retreat of the remaining glaciers, by the invisibly slow erosion from wind pounding against the mountains, by the dramatic roar and rip of yearly avalanches reshaping the mountainsides, and by the legions of mountain streams slicing gorges such as Sunrift, Hidden Falls, and Avalanche Creek ever deeper as the waters rush headlong into the Flathead and St. Mary rivers.

Today's Glaciers

Today's glaciers are not the massive ice age glaciers that carved the park's landscape. They are much younger—and they are disappearing.

During the recent Little Ice Age, which began around 1550 and reached its peak in 1850, there were vast expanses of snow and ice fields and more than 150 glaciers in the park. Since 1850, a mere blink of

an eye in geological time, the glaciers have steadily receded. At press time, only twenty-seven glaciers remain. The largest and most impressive of these are Agassiz, Grinnell, Sperry, Harrison, Rainbow, Blackfoot, and Jackson glaciers. According to park officials, most of the glaciers have shrunk to between one-half and one-third their size in the last 100 years. Other glaciers have disappeared.

George Bird Grinnell, dubbed "the father of modern conservation," described Grinnell Glacier, named in his honor, this way in 1888: "The glacier was vocal with the sound of running water. The musical tinkle of the tiny rivulet, the deep bass roar of the dashing torrent, the hiss of rushing water, confined as in a flume, fell upon the ear, and through the holes and crevasse in the ice came strange hollow murmurs, growlings and roarings."

When George Bird Grinnell died in 1938 at age eighty-nine, the New York Times *called Grinnell "the father of American conservation."*
Courtesy Glacier National Park Archives.

The strange, hollow murmur of the dying glaciers continues. According to USGS Northern Rocky Mountain Science Center ecologist Dan Fagre, at the present rate of melting, all the glaciers in the park will be gone by the year 2030.

Piikáni camp on Cut Bank Creek in the early 1900s.
Courtesy Kramer Gallery, Minneapolis, Minnesota.

The Native Tribes of the Northern Rocky Mountains

ARCHEOLOGICAL EVIDENCE SUGGESTS *the first people came to the area that includes what is now Glacier National Park approximately 10,000 years ago—perhaps longer. They occupied these lands seasonally, depending on the climate, the geological processes at work, and the movement of the bison, bighorn sheep, and mule deer, which appear to have been the favored game of those long-ago people.*

Throughout the millennia various tribes—including the Cree, the Háninin (Atsina or Gros Ventre), the Nakota (Assiniboine and Stoneys),

the Pend d'Oreille (Upper Kalispel), and the Bitterroot Salish (Flathead)—were known to enter the mountains we now call Glacier National Park. The tribes that had the longest continuing presence, exceeding 1,000 years, were the Niitsitapi (Real People), commonly known as the Blackfoot Confederacy or the Blackfeet, and the K'tunaxa (k-too-nah-ha) (The People), commonly known as the Kutenai, which is an older spelling of the name (generally spelled Kootenay in Canada and Kootenai in the United States).

The Niitsitapi (Blackfoot Confederacy)

In the mid-1700s Niitsitapi warriors mounted on fine, fast horses laid claim to the northern Great Plains. For the next 100 years they controlled all the lands east of the Continental Divide from the North Saskatchewan River south to the Missouri and Musselshell rivers and east to the Sweetgrass (Blood

Clot) Hills; they roamed and raided as far south as the Yellowstone River.

The Niitsitapi guarded the passes across the Rocky Mountains to keep western tribes—the K'tunaxa, Nez Perce, Pend d'Oreille, and Salish—from crossing the mountains to hunt bison in territory they claimed as their own. They fought tribes from the east and south—the Cree, Sioux, and their once-mightiest enemies the Shoshone and Absaroke (Crow)—to keep them from invading the beaver- and bison-rich country from the Musselshell River to the Saskatchewan River. They fought and then welcomed fur traders. However, the Niitsitapi's reputation as fierce warriors kept Canadian and American fur traders from the part of the Rocky Mountains that would someday become Glacier National Park well into the 1800s.

There are three tribes of the Niitsitapi: The northernmost tribe, the Siksiká (Blackfoot), ranged the

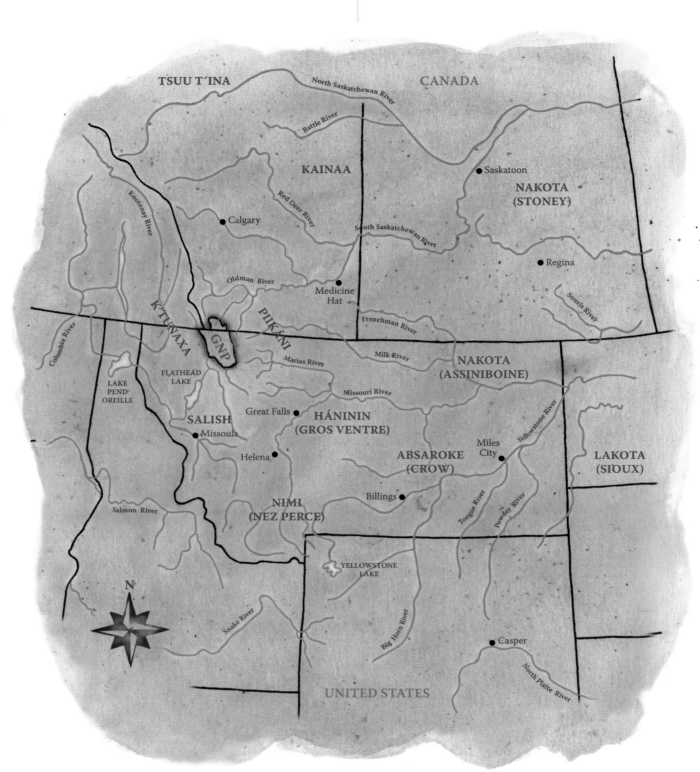

Tribes of the northern Great Plains.
Original mapping from 2001 report titled "Our Mountains are our Pillows" by Dr. Brian Reeves and Dr. Sandra Peacock. Courtesy Glacier National Park.

parklands and plains of the North Saskatchewan River; the Kainaa (the Bloods or Many Chiefs) inhabited the area from the Red Deer River east along the South Saskatchewan River and beyond the Cypress Hills; and the Piikáni (Piegan or Peigan) ranged from the Bow River south to the Missouri River and east as far as the Sweetgrass Hills.

American fur traders were the first to use the terms Blackfoot and Blackfeet to refer to all three tribes of the Niitsitapi, as well as the Háninin (Atsina or Gros Ventre) and the Tsuu T'ina (Sarci). Canadian fur trappers called them by their tribal names. The United States government began to use the terms Blackfoot and Blackfeet in 1851, when the U.S. Treaty of Fort Laramie identified the Niitsitapi as the Blackfoot Nation.

The Piikáni are the most numerous of the three tribes—their numbers exceeding 15,000 at least twice in early history. There are two divisions of Piikáni: the North Piikáni and the South Piikáni. Although both divisions of the Piikáni ranged from the Bow River south to the Missouri River, the North Piikáni favored wintering in the Porcupine Hills and Oldman River Valley in what is now Alberta, Canada. The South Piikáni are the Indians most associated with today's Glacier National Park. They often wintered in the foothills on the eastern slopes of Glacier's mountains, on the shores of St. Mary Lakes (North and South Inside lakes), at the foot of Lower and Two Medicine

Hunting buffalo near the Sweetgrass Hills.
Archives and Special Collections, The University of Montana–Missoula.

For more than 100 years, Niitsitapi warriors guarded the passes of the northern Rocky Mountains. They kept other tribes from the bison hunting grounds of the Great Plains and hampered the exploration of the Northwest by Europeans. Explorer and road builder Lt. John Mullan referred to them as "these hellhounds of the mountains."
Blackfoot Indian on Horseback, Karl Bodmer, 1840. Courtesy Beinecke Rare Book and Manuscript Library, Yale University.

lakes, up Cut Bank Creek, and on Apikuni Flats. They also wintered in the wooded bottomlands along the Marias (Bear) River tributary of the Missouri (Big) River east of the mountains.

The Piikáni generally used South Kootenay (Where-the-K´tunaxa-Go-Up) Pass in today's Waterton Lakes National Park, Cut Bank Pass in what is now Glacier National Park, and Marias (Medicine) Pass on the southern border of Glacier for traveling back and forth across the Rocky Mountains. These passes were connected by trails to the Old North Trail east of the park. The Old North Trail was used by nearly all Native Americans since time immemorial for traveling north and south along the eastern flanks of the Rocky Mountains.

In the Piikáni traditional religion, the Rocky Mountains—known as the Backbone (Mistakis) by the Piikáni—are their most sacred place. They are a place of power where plants used as medicine or in spiritual ceremonies are found. They are also where sacred animals come from, including grizzlies, wolves, eagles, and ravens. Many sacred rituals are held there,

Family gathering at a Piikáni encampment.
Walter McClintock, circa 1900. Courtesy Beinecke Rare Book and Manuscript Library, Yale University.

Piikáni and Sioux warriors battle over the bison hunting grounds in the long and bloody Indian wars of the 1860s.
Blackfeet and Sioux, C. M. Russell, 1908. Courtesy Sid Richardson Museum, Fort Worth, Texas.

the Beaver Bundle and Medicine Pipe ceremonies among the most important.

The Beaver Bundle is the most ancient of the religious bundles. Made from animal hides, bundles contained sacred objects and were used in religious ceremonies related to calling the bison and planting and harvesting sacred tobacco. Each Niitsitapi tribe had a Beaver Bundle, and all were derived from the first bundle. According to Siksiká elders White Head Calf, Old Bull, and Many Guns in the 1930s, and the 2001 studies of Dr. Brian Reeves and Dr. Sandra Peacock in

a report titled "Our Mountains are Our Pillows: An Ethnographic Overview of Glacier National Park," it appears that today's Waterton Lakes National Park is the place of origin of the Beaver Bundle.

The Medicine Pipe Bundles are kept by spiritual leaders and have been passed on for centuries. These bundles are the gifts of Thunder, who lives in the Rocky Mountains. Brings-Down-the-Sun, the elder spiritual leader of the North Piikáni, told author/photographer Walter McClintock in 1905 that Thunder lives in a cave near the summit of Chief Mountain

(Ninastakis), and this belief is generally shared by Piikáni elders.

One ritual often held in the Glacier portion of the Rocky Mountains is the vision quest, a ritual performed only by men. The vision seeker carried a blanket, sweetgrass, and tobacco offerings and climbed to

A group of Niitsitapi men and women travel on horseback, several pulling travois.
The Trail Makers, Roland Reed, circa 1912. Library of Congress, Prints and Photographs Division. LC-US262-46941.

the vision quest site. He fasted and prayed for four days and nights, awaiting his vision, which came the last night. Favored vision quest sites included Two Medicine and Chief Mountain.

Although the Piikáni traditionally held their midsummer medicine lodge (Okan) eastward along the Milk (Little) and Marias rivers toward the Sweetgrass Hills, it was at least once held at Two Medicine Lake—in the 1830s, according to fur trapper Hugh Monroe.

The Changing World of the Niitsitapi
The last 300 years were a time of great change for the Niitsitapi. They experienced three events that profoundly changed their world: the introduction of the horse, the arrival of fur traders, and the westward expansion of the United States.

The Horse
Before the Niitsitapi acquired horses, they moved their winter camps to the sheltering foothills and their summer camps to the game-rich plains in packs or on travois harnessed to dogs. Before they had horses, they hunted bison on foot. The hunts were limited by how far they could travel and by how much bison

meat the dogs could carry.

In 1732 the Piikáni tribe of the Niitsitapi was attacked by an enemy tribe, either the Absaroke (Crow) or the Shoshone, near the Red Deer River. The enemy warriors were mounted on fast horses, which usually gave them a decided advantage in battle. But by that time the Piikáni were well armed with guns from Canadian fur traders and were able to defeat their once mighty enemies.

The Piikáni kept the horses of their slain enemies. They called the strange animals Big Dogs or Elk Dogs. One Big Dog could carry as much meat and as many hides and utensils as six or seven dogs, and it could carry a man wherever he wanted to go as swift as the wind. The Big Dogs gave them the ability to easily follow the roaming bison vast distances, to quickly move their villages to new hunting grounds, and to raid and plunder rival tribes with stealth and speed. During the next twenty years, the Niitsitapi horse herds grew—both by breeding and by taking horses from

rival tribes. By 1754 large herds of fine horses—born of Arabian, Andalusian, and Barb bloodlines, descendants of the first Spanish horses brought to this continent—grazed the northern Great Plains and carried Niitsitapi warriors to the hunt and into battle. Thus began the Niitsitapi's hundred-year reign.

The Niitsitapi lived by the bison; the great beasts were their main source of meat. All parts of the bison were used for a variety of purposes: hides formed the walls of their tepees, and made winter coats, swaddling for babies, moccasins, robes, and parfleches (bags). The paunch was used as a cooking pot and the bladder for carrying water; sinews became thread; and bones made scrapers, knives, and awls. The fur was woven into ropes or used to stuff cradleboards.
Indians Hunting the Bison, Karl Bodmer, 1839. Courtesy Beinecke Rare Book and Manuscript Library, Yale University.

The Fur Trade

The Siksiká, Kainaa, and Piikáni tribes had been trading indirectly with the French and British since the late 1600s, after the beaver populations in the eastern provinces of Canada had been depleted by trappers. Cree and Assiniboine middlemen brought canoe loads of iron arrowheads, metal tools, utensils, cloth, tobacco, and eventually powder and guns from the French posts on the St. Lawrence River and the British York Factory on Hudson Bay to trade for pelts with the tribes of the still beaver-rich western provinces. The

*Piikáni village
on the Plains.*
Walter McClintock, circa 1900.
Courtesy Beinecke Rare Book and
Manuscript Library, Yale University.

Cree and Assiniboine middlemen then paddled their fur-laden canoes back to the French and British posts and traded for more goods.

Although the system worked well for years, in 1733 British fur traders began building trading posts in the Saskatchewan in order to trade directly with the Siksiká, Kainaa, and the North and South Piikáni. By 1780 the Piikáni were regularly taking their own furs the long distances to the Saskatchewan trading posts. These long treks to trade their furs continued until 1831, when the American Fur Company built Fort Piegan, the first trading post in Piikáni territory at the confluence of the Marias and Missouri rivers.

The fur trade that brought the welcomed tobacco, iron pots, blankets, whiskey, and guns to the Niitsitapi also brought smallpox epidemics that decimated their populations. In addition, it armed their enemies and brought non-Indian settlement to their territory.

The Westward Expansion of the United States

Although Niitsitapi warriors fought with the zeal of Roman conquerors to protect their traditional hunting ranges on the northern Great Plains, their world

would change and shrink in the mid–1800s by a force they could not stop: the power and resolve of the emerging nation to the east, the United States.

Beginning in the 1840s the United States began exercising its ownership of the lands acquired through the Louisiana Purchase. A constant stream of determined pioneers answered the siren call of gold, silver, timber, grasslands, and rich farm soils and rolled their wagons westward. Piikáni warriors were spread thin as they tried to turn the advancing tide of settlers away from their territory, while also fighting to keep the K'tunaxa, Salish, Cree, Absaroke, and Sioux out of their bison hunting grounds.

Other forces to be reckoned with were on the horizon. In 1845 the U.S. Congress began discussing the idea of a transcontinental railroad to unite the East with the West. In 1855 Congress authorized the U.S. Army to survey possible routes for the railroad. The task fell to Washington Territorial Governor Isaac Stevens.

Stevens' first order of business was to define the hunting grounds of the Piikáni in an attempt to halt the tribal wars over the bison hunting ranges. The Indian wars were a continuing threat to settlers and survey teams—and to future railroad builders.

A treaty was drawn up to designate the Piikáni hunting grounds. The treaty, known by the Piikáni as the Lame Bull Treaty, described their hunting range as "a large area following the main divide of the Rocky Mountains from the 49th parallel [U.S./Canada border] south and east to the sources of the Yellowstone, and down as far as Twenty-five Yard Creek where it struck north to the Musselshell." The treaty defined the area as the exclusive reserve of the Piikáni for the next ninety-nine years. It included land now in Glacier National Park east of the Continental Divide.

The Lame Bull Treaty with the Piikáni enraged the Absaroke, Sioux, and other Plains tribes, and the bloody war over the bison hunting grounds that had raged since the mid-1700s continued. This more than 100-year war finally came to an end in 1870 when the exhausted warriors of all the tribes fought their last battle at Oldman River in Alberta, Canada. For the next ten years the Niitsitapi lived a strained yet peaceful existence with their neighboring tribes.

The nomadic ways of the Niitsitapi were irretrievably changed with the loss of their hunting lands.

The 1870 massacre of Piikáni leader Heavy Runner and his village by U.S. troops and the near extinction of the bison in the 1880s delivered the final blows. The proud nations of the Niitsitapi reluctantly moved onto reservations in Montana and Canada. The Siksiká now reside on the Siksiká Nation east of Calgary; the Kainaa live on the Blood Reserve in southern Alberta; the North Piikáni reside on the Peigan Nation in southwestern Alberta; and the South Piikáni live on the Blackfeet Reservation in Montana on the eastern border of Glacier National Park. The South Piikáni now officially refer to themselves as the Blackfeet.

The K´tunaxa (Kootenai)

Although the Piikáni are the Indians most often associated with today's Glacier National Park, the K´tunaxa (Kutenai, Kootenay, Kootenai) seasonally occupied the western slopes of the mountains of what is now Glacier National Park for at least a thousand

years and traveled east over the passes to hunt bison. The K´tunaxa, just as the Piikáni, had sacred sites in the mountains and a strong and enduring attachment to Glacier.

The origins of the K´tunaxa are a mystery. They speak a language unlike any other and there is no known ancestral language. They have lived in the Kootenai and Columbia River valleys of the Rocky Mountain Trench for thousands of years. There are two divisions of the K´tunaxa. The Upper K´tunaxa occupied the upper reaches of the Kootenai River, the headwaters of the Columbia River, the Columbia Lakes region, and the Rocky Mountain valleys to the east. The Lower K´tunaxa occupied the lower reaches of the Kootenai River below Kootenai Falls and the Kootenai Lakes.

Three bands of the K´tunaxa were traditionally associated with the area that is now Waterton Lakes National Park and Glacier National Park: the

The K'tunaxa developed the maneuverable sturgeon-nosed canoe with a reverse prow to travel through the bulrushes and turbulent waters of rivers and streams.
Archives and Special Collections, The University of Montana–Missoula.

Gakawakamitukinik (Raven's Nest), Akanahonek (Tobacco Plains), and the Akiyinik (Jennings) bands. The Raven's Nest band hunted bison along the eastern foothills between Oldman River and today's Waterton Lakes and Glacier national parks. They wintered on the eastern slopes of the Rocky Mountains in the area of Crowsnest Pass until the smallpox epidemic of 1732, which nearly destroyed the band. Those who survived moved west to join the bands on the Tobacco Plains. The Jennings band lived on the Kootenai River in the vicinity of the old town of Jennings, a mile upstream of present-day Libby, Montana. They moved to the Kalispell, Montana, area in the early 1850s.

Piikáni men rest their horses at a water hole near Swiftcurrent Pass.
The Water Hole, Roland Reed, early 1900s. Courtesy Kramer Gallery, Minneapolis, Minnesota.

This band seasonally joined with the Salish and Pend d'Oreille to use Marias Pass to cross the mountains to hunt bison.

The K'tunaxa band most associated with Glacier is the Akanahonek (Tobacco Plains) band that wintered in the Tobacco Plains east of the Kootenai River near the Montana/British Columbia boundary. They were mountain and lake people, who generally used canoes for transportation, and they were proud of their skills as hunters, trappers, and fishermen. They seasonally camped on the shores of Waterton Lakes (known by them as Long Lake, Lake Cut in Two, and Smooth-Even-Sized-Pebble-Beach) and Lake McDonald (Place-

of-Dancing) along the western slopes of the mountains to hunt game and to fish and trap in the rivers and streams. They picked berries and dug medicinal and edible plants in the mountains and meadows and performed their traditional sacred rituals. (Chief Mountain and the foot of Lake McDonald are sacred sites to the K´tunaxa.) Three times a year they traveled over the mountains to the eastern slopes to hunt bison. They camped at the St. Mary and Two Medicine lakes.

Before the K´tunaxa acquired horses, they only went eastward for bison in the winter when the snows were deep, because it was easier to haul the heavy packs of meat over the mountains and there was less chance of conflict with the Piikáni. They traveled on snowshoes over South Kootenay Pass (Buffalo [Cow] Trail), Swiftcurrent Pass, and Logan (Packs-Pulled-Up) Pass. They hunted sheep and other game on the way, and then bison on the eastern slopes of Waterton and Glacier. In the winter the bison migrated to the sheltering foothills, and the K´tunaxa did not have to venture far onto the plains to get their supply of meat. Once they acquired horses, they continued their winter hunts on snowshoes, but they also traveled eastward for bison in the spring and fall on horses.

The K´tunaxa and the Niitsitapi appear to have been friendly until the 1700s. Archeological evidence indicates that both groups occupied the foot of Wa-

terton Lakes, although not necessarily in the same winters. In the 1730s both cultures acquired horses. During that same period both of their populations were decimated by smallpox epidemics. As their populations recovered, they became enemies—fighting over hunting territory and the declining supply of beaver and bison.

Like the Niitsitapi, the nomadic ways of the K´tunaxa changed irretrievably in 1855 with the United States' westward expansion and the coming of the railroads. Washington Territorial Governor Isaac Stevens persuaded the Lower K´tunaxa to join with the Bitterroot Salish and Upper Pend d'Oreille to form a confederation and live on a reservation. The reservation was established in the Mission Valley in Montana. The tribes agreed, and their territories within the United States, which included what is now the west side of Glacier National Park, became open for settle-

Indians on the old Travois Trail, Glacier National Park, Montana.

Postcards circa 1914 depict Indians living in Glacier National Park.
Courtesy Tom Mulvaney.

ment. Some K´tunaxa moved to the Flathead Reservation, but most went north to their ancestral lands on the Tobacco Plains.

Today there are seven bands of the K´tunaxa: five in British Columbia and two in the United States. (In the United States the bands are called tribes.) The Confederated Salish and Kootenai are near Elmo, Montana, and the Kootenai Tribe of Idaho is in Bonner's Ferry. The bands residing in Canada prefer to be known as the K´tunaxa.

Free Trapper.
Charles M. Russell. Oil on canvas, 1911.
Excerpted from *Free Trapper.*
Courtesy of the Montana Historical Society
Doug O'looney photographer 9/1987

3

The Fur Trade Comes West

Rich in resources, *the northern Rocky Mountains, including what are now Glacier and Waterton Lakes national parks, began drawing fur traders from the East and from Europe in the 1700s and early 1800s. Unlike in eastern North America, the region's beaver populations were still abundant, and forts and trading posts began appearing throughout the Northwest. The result was a clash between fur traders and Indian tribes for land and economic opportunity.*

The French and British Clash

The fuss over fur began when French navigator Jacques Cartier traveled up the St. Lawrence River on his quest to find the Northwest Passage to the Pacific Ocean in 1535—and in the process, accidentally launched the 300-year-long era of the fur trade. Cartier's river route from the Atlantic Ocean was blocked by unnavigable rapids at what is now Montreal, Canada. Stuck in the wilderness, Cartier, ever the entrepreneur, began trading knives and iron kettles with the Iroquois for whatever they had to offer—including beaver pelts, which he shipped to Europe. Hat makers discovered that the pelts made excellent felt, and soon these furs were in great demand. The French reacted to the increased demand by recruiting Indians as commercial trappers. Business boomed until the early 1600s, when the supply of beavers in the east was trapped out and the fur trade shifted westward.

As French trade spread throughout the region, a rivalry brewed between the French and the British for domination of North America and its resources. British navigator Henry Hudson sailed through a strait from the Labrador Sea into a great bay in Northeastern Canada. He named it Hudson Bay and set up a trading post at the southern end of the bay in 1668, calling it Hudson's Bay Company.

For the next eight decades the French and British skirmished over possession of land and the fur trade until war broke out in 1754. The French and Indian War lasted until 1763, when the British armies defeated the French and all of the French possessions in North America were turned over to the British.

The Nor'Westers

After the war, the British assumed they would take over the fur trade—but they did not take into account the ambitious French-Canadian and Scottish free-traders in Montreal, who in 1775 formed the North West Fur Trading Company. Calling themselves Nor'Westers, these aggressive adventurers explored west and set up trading posts from Montreal to the Pacific Ocean. A fierce competition for furs between Hudson's Bay traders and the Nor'Westers ensued.

Under the leadership of Welch surveyor and mapmaker David Thompson, the Nor'Westers explored much of what would later be described as the American Northwest. They traveled far northern routes to avoid the wrath of the Siksiká, Kainaa, and Piikáni who guarded the passes over the mountains of what are now Glacier and Waterton Lakes national parks. Thompson established trading posts near what is now Libby, Montana, at Kullyspell House near Lake Pend Oreille in Idaho, and at Saleesh House near Thompson Falls, Montana.

In a wilderness game of tic-tac-toe, the Hudson's Bay Company and the Nor'Westers covered the western frontier with trading posts. The competition for the fur trade between these two companies lasted nearly half a century. In the end the Nor'Westers won the battle for territory and the two companies merged under the name of Hudson Bay Company in 1821.

The adventurous fur trappers were the first non-Indians to journey into Piikáni territory and explore the rugged land that is now Glacier National Park.
Beaver Furs, Mark Ogle. Courtesy Mark Ogle Studios, Kalispell, Montana.

Chief Mountain: Photo by Tony Bynum

Peter Fidler

In 1792 the Hudson's Bay Company sent surveyor Peter Fidler to map the area just east of the Rocky Mountains. Fidler wintered with the Piikáni on the slopes east of what is now Glacier National Park. He is not known to have entered the mountains, but he gave the region its first English place name when he labeled Kings Mountain on his map, which was printed in 1795. The name was later changed to Chief Mountain, which is known by the Piikáni as Ninastakis and by the K'tunaxa as Nahsukin.

The American Fur Traders

While the fur traders from Canada were pressing south, in 1803 U.S. President Thomas Jefferson negotiated the purchase of the vast French-owned Louisiana Territory, which began at the Mississippi River and extended as far west as present-day Montana, Wyoming, Colorado, and New Mexico. As soon as the ink was dry on the Louisiana Purchase, President Jefferson sent Captains Meriwether Lewis and William Clark and the Corps of Discovery to explore the newly acquired lands.

When Lewis and Clark returned to St. Louis after their epic journey of 1803 to 1806, they told of the beaver-rich regions of the Upper Missouri River. On the strength of Lewis and Clark's report, Manuel Lisa of St. Louis,

who was then trading with the Osage, predicted that a fortune awaited the men who could tap the yet untouched fur sources on the Upper Missouri. In 1807 he organized the first American fur company on the Upper Missouri: the St. Louis Missouri Fur Company. It was reorganized as the Missouri Fur Company in 1812. The company built the first trading post in

Beaver on the Upper Missouri River in the early 1800s.
Karl Bodmer, 1809. Courtesy Rare Books Division, The New York Public Library. Astor Lenox and Tilder Foundation.

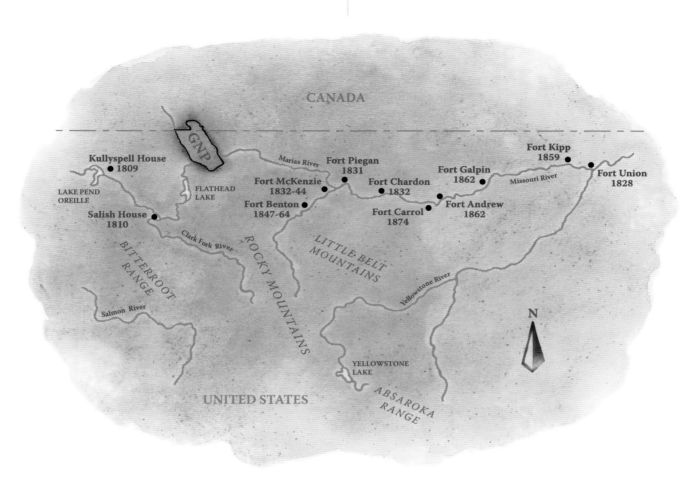

CANADA

Kullyspell House
● 1809

LAKE PEND
OREILLE

FLATHEAD
LAKE

Salish House
1810

Marias River

Fort Piegan
1831

Fort McKenzie
1832-44

Fort Benton
1847-64

Fort Chardon
● 1832

Fort Carrol
1874

Fort Andrew
1862

Fort Galpin
1862 ●

Fort Kipp
1859 ●

Missouri River

Fort Union
1828

Clark Fork River

ROCKY MOUNTAINS

BITTERROOT RANGE

Salmon River

LITTLE BELT
MOUNTAINS

Yellowstone River

N

YELLOWSTONE
LAKE

UNITED STATES

ABSAROKA
RANGE

Trading posts west of Glacier National Park and east along the Upper Missouri River.

Montana—Fort Ramon at the junction of the Bighorn and Yellowstone rivers—and set out to capture the beaver-rich Upper Missouri region fur trade, a major portion of which was in the traditional range of the Piikáni.

Although the Piikáni traded with the Hudson's Bay Company and the Nor'Westers, they were hostile toward the American fur trading companies until the late 1820s. Their refusal to trade with the Americans was partly at the urging of the Hudson's Bay Company and partly because the Americans, who had established posts in the territory of the Absaroke (Crow), were providing Piikáni enemies with guns. Manuel Lisa's St. Louis Missouri Fur Company added to the bad blood with the tribes when he began employing non-Indian trappers—later renowned as "mountain men"—rather than relying on Indians as the sole source for pelts.

As the fur trade expanded closer to the Rocky Mountains, the Americans encountered increasing numbers of hostile Indians, which included the Háninin (Gros Ventre), Absaroke, Nakota (Assiniboine), Siksiká, Kainaa, and Piikáni.

Expanding the Fur Trade into Piikáni Territory
Despite persistent clashes with tribes, American fur traders continued to expand their territories.

John Jacob Astor founded the American Fur Company in the Midwest and Pacific Northwest in 1808. By the 1820s the company had expanded its trade into the Rocky Mountains and Great Plains. It promptly merged with the Missouri Fur Company and then swallowed up most of the other fur companies that had organized on the Upper Missouri.

Kenneth MacKenzie, who ran the Upper Missouri fur trade for the American Fur Company in 1831, was the first to expand the American fur trade into Piikáni territory. MacKenzie sent his trusted agent James Kipp to establish trade with these monarchs of the northern Great Plains at the mouth of the Marias River on the flanks of the Rocky Mountains.

Kipp and his party of seventy-five men boarded a keelboat laden with trade goods at Fort Union on the mouth of the Yellowstone River and slowly made their way up the Missouri to the Marias River. As soon as they tied up the keelboat, the Piikáni came to trade. Kipp was fearful that his men had little protection

James Kipp.
Circa 1830s.
Courtesy Overholser
Historical Research Center,
Fort Benton, Montana.

from the potentially hostile Piikáni and managed to persuade the Indians to leave while he constructed a trading post. Seventy-five days later Kipp's men had constructed storerooms, a trade room, and living quarters. The compound of buildings was surrounded by twenty-five-foot-tall cottonwood pickets for protection, and a cannon was installed in one corner. Named Fort Piegan, the post only survived one trading season. When it was time to return to Fort Union for the winter, none of Kipp's men would stay in Piikáni territory. As soon as the traders were gone, the Indians burned the fort.

The next spring, undaunted by the uncertainties of trade with a tribe they believed to be hostile, the American Fur Company constructed Fort MacKenzie six miles upstream from the ruins of Fort Piegan. This time the Piikáni were anxious to trade, and Fort MacKenzie prospered until 1844. That year it was abandoned when factor Frances A. Chardon ordered an attack on a party of Siksiká in revenge for the killing of a fort employee by a previous trading party. The next day, Chardon, fearing reprisal, ordered Fort Mackenzie abandoned and began constructing Fort Chardon at the mouth of the Judith River.

Other forts along the Upper Missouri were built, then burned or were abandoned; a few prospered and became cities such as Fort Benton, downriver from Fort MacKenzie.

The demand for beaver pelts lasted until 1840. By then the beaver populations in North America were severely depleted, and silk hats had replaced fur as the fashion in Europe. The beaver fur trade was replaced by an energetic trade in bison hides for lap robes that continued until the bison herds were hunted nearly to extinction in the 1880s.

A keelboat is cordelled upstream. Approximately fifteen to twenty men would wade ashore and pull the keelboat upstream with a towline, known as a "cordelle." The men on shore had to walk through underbrush and across bluffs to drag the boat along. By cordelling, poling, and sailing, they moved the boat upstream.
Karl Bodmer, circa 1831.
Courtesy Missouri Historical Society and Overholser Historical Research Center, Fort Benton, Montana.

Mountain Man Hugh Monroe

Hugh Monroe is believed to be the first non-Indian to extensively explore the mountains and valleys of what is now Glacier National Park. He was born in Quebec in 1798, the son of a British Army captain and a French woman whose family had been among the first French families to arrive in Canada following explorer Jacques Cartier's launching of the fur trade in the mid-1500s.

Monroe joined the Hudson's Bay Company in 1815 and was assigned to Edmonton House on the Saskatchewan River. During his apprenticeship he became a skilled trapper and savvy trader. He also had an abiding interest in the Indians and a knack for learning their languages. In 1823 he was sent to live with the Inuk´sik (Small Robes) band of the Piikáni to learn their language, keep an eye on the progress of the American traders, scout for beaver trapping areas, and make sure the Indians delivered their furs to the Hudson Bay posts. The Inuk´sik traditionally wintered on the eastern slopes of Glacier's mountains.

The Piikáni elder Rising Head agreed to be Monroe's guardian to ensure his safety among the Piikáni. Monroe lived and worked with Rising Head's band for some time and learned the ways of the Piikáni. He later joined Lone Walker's band and married Lone Walker's daughter, Mink Woman. It was on a raid with Lone Walker's band against the Crow that Monroe proved he was a

Hugh Monroe.
Circa 1880s. Donor J. E. A. MacLeod, Calgary, CA.
Courtesy Montana Historical Society

fearless warrior and earned his Piikáni name: Rising Wolf.

Content with his new life, Monroe left the Hudson Bay Company and trapped for the American Fur Company. He worked as a free-trapper, camping on the plains and in what are now the St. Mary and Two Medicine valleys of Glacier until his death in 1892.

Monroe was legendary among early explorers and settlers. He was a great storyteller and, when it suited him, a congenial guide and interpreter. Monroe claimed he guided the Jesuit missionary Pierre-Jean DeSmet across the mountains, and together they christened the walled-in lakes east of the Continental Divide St. Mary. However, there is no record that Monroe and DeSmet ever actually met. During DeSmet's travels in the country west of the Continental Divide, he converted the Kootenai to Catholicism and erected wooden crosses in elaborate ceremonies with the tribes. The popular though questionable story is that Monroe and a band of K'tunaxa erected a cross of logs on the shore and christened the lakes St. Mary.

Monroe found his place in history guiding author James Willard Schultz around future Glacier National Park in the 1870s. He is credited with providing Schultz with a wealth of information about the Piikáni that Schultz later used to write several books about the park. Monroe was immortalized by Schultz in the book *Rising Wolf, The White Blackfeet* about Monroe's life with the Piikáni.

Workers pose for the camera as Great Northern officials drive the ceremonial last spike in the Cascade Mountains to complete the nation's fifth transcontinental railroad on January 6, 1893. Many of these men will stay to farm and build towns in the Northwest.

4

Exploration and Settlement from the East

T HE FUR TRADE *brought the first non-Indians to the northern Rocky Mountains and opened up the area that would become Glacier National Park to be explored, claimed, chronicled, and settled. Following in the footsteps of the fur traders were the miners and settlers seeking new lands, riches, or simply a better way of life. As their wagons rolled westward, the borders of the fledgling United States began to take shape.*

Drawing the Line

While the adventuresome trappers, traders, and mountain men were exploring the country for fur, a greater issue was brewing—territorial boundaries of the U.S. and British-owned Canada.

The northern branches of the Missouri River were considered the northern boundary of the French-owned Louisiana Territory. When the United States purchased those lands in 1803, the Americans and British were satisfied with the division of territories—except for the rather dramatic southward dip in the border as the Missouri flowed east toward the Mississippi River. The issue was settled in an 1818 treaty between Britain and the United States that established the U.S./Canada border at the forty-ninth parallel from Lake Superior to the east face of the Rocky Mountains. But ownership of what would become Glacier National Park was still far from settled.

Sensing the intensity of the border disputes, in 1837 the U.S. Congress sent Department of State translator and librarian Robert Greenhow to make a report on the discovery of the Northwest Coast of North America. The report was published in 1840, the maps in 1845. His maps were compiled from a multitude of sources—including accounts of Indians and trappers—and were remarkably complete. The maps identified lakes, streams, tribal lands, and trading posts, and they marked a "route across the mountains" that later would inspire a quest to find this promising pass that could open up the Northwest to the railroad.

Fifty-Four Forty or Fight

The land west of the Rocky Mountains to the Pacific Ocean—except for the Spanish holdings from the forty-second parallel south—was unclaimed. In the Northwest, this included present-day Washington, Oregon, Idaho, and parts of Montana and Wyoming—as well as everything west of the Continental Divide in today's Glacier National Park and a good chunk of northwestern Canada.

British and American fur traders and politicians scrambled to claim ownership of these open territories. The British wanted the boundary west of the

Robert Greenhow's 1845 map of the west coast of North America.
Manuscripts, Archives, and Special Collections, Washington State University Libraries WSU479.

Rockies fixed at the forty-sixth parallel. The Americans argued the border should be farther north, at the fifty-fourth parallel (54°40'), giving birth to the slogan Fifty-Four Forty or Fight. The whole matter would not be settled until 1846, when President James K. Polk accepted the British offer to extend the border from the Rocky Mountains to the coast at the forty-ninth parallel.

The Piikáni Sell
Although the land disputes between the United States and Britain in Canada were settled, the land east of the Continental Divide that is now part of Glacier National Park still had another owner—the Piikáni (Blackfeet). They had long ago claimed it as their territory. Their claim was acknowledged by the United States in the 1851 Fort Laramie Treaty and would remain as Piikáni territory until 1895, when the elders of the tribe agreed to sell the land to the United States.

A Route across the Rockies
The United States was eager to build the first transcontinental railroad and was aggressively searching

for routes across the Rocky Mountains to the Pacific Ocean in the 1800s. The need for these routes fueled the exploration of the West and of the Glacier area. In 1853 three reconnaissance surveying parties headed west. The largest and best equipped was the Northern Trail survey party, which was charged with exploring the Great Lakes to Puget Sound. It was led by then governor of Washington Territory Isaac I. Stevens. The Piikáni knew the easiest pass across the mountains, and Greenhow had mapped it from their accounts in 1840. Governor Stevens sent engineer A. W. Tinkham to find it.

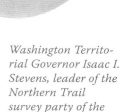

The Secret Pass
Tinkham and a Salish scout started on the western side of the Rocky Mountains, traveling north through the Flathead Valley, then east. They followed an old Indian trail up Nyack Creek and crossed the Continental Divide at the 7,600 feet elevation of Cut Bank Pass. It was October and three degrees above zero. Tinkham, shivering from the cold, fearing the Piikáni, and believing he had just crossed the long-sought pass, came down from the mountains and hurried to Fort Benton to make his report to Governor Stevens. He described the pass as "narrow, wooded and precipitous, with a bare rocky ridge offering foothold for a horse, but by no means practicable for the passage of wagons."

Stevens was not satisfied with Tinkham's report. Piikáni Chief Little Dog had described the pass to him earlier, and it was far different than Tinkham's description. The following spring Stevens sent engineer James Doty to look for the pass from the eastern side. Doty's scout was mountain man Hugh Monroe. Doty and Monroe explored the front range, passed the trail that Tinkham had traveled, went north toward what is now Lower St. Mary Lake, then turned south to explore an old Indian trail. They entered the mountains through a gap fifteen miles wide. Doty believed he had found the east entrance to the pass and jubilantly sent word to Stevens. But by then Jefferson Davis, who was in charge of the survey parties as a member of President Franklin Pierce's cabinet and would later

Washington Territorial Governor Isaac I. Stevens, leader of the Northern Trail survey party of the Northern Railroad Survey 1853 to 1855.
Archives and Special Collections, The University of Montana–Missoula and Burlington Northern–Santa Fe Railway.

become president of the Confederate states, favored a southern railroad route. He sent Stevens a message to stop any further search for the mysterious pass. The northern passage was abandoned as a possible route for the nation's first transcontinental railroad. The elusive pass would remain a Piikáni secret another thirty-five years.

The Pass is Found

It wasn't until 1889, when James J. Hill's Great Northern Railway was laying track across Montana to the Pacific Ocean to build the nation's fifth transcontinental railroad, that the location of the mysterious pass—already known to the Indians—was finally discovered by a non-Indian.

Hill hired thirty-six-year-old John F. Stevens to find the pass. Stevens had worked his way up from surveying team axman and rodman to location engineer. He had helped lay the routes for the Milwaukee, the Duluth, and the Canadian Pacific railroads and planned the route of the Denver and Rio Grande narrow-gauge railroad. He was known as the best mountain-country location engineer in the nation.

In December 1889 Stevens set out from Fort Assin-

Great Northern Railway location engineer John F. Stevens. Circa 1913.

Archives and Special Collections, The University of Montana–Missoula and Burlington Northern–Santa Fe Railway.

niboine with a wagon, a mule, and a saddle horse. He traveled 160 miles to the Blackfeet Agency to hire a guide, but no Blackfeet would agree to take him to the pass.

At the time Stevens arrived, the once proud rulers of the plains had suffered the effects of smallpox, the trader's whiskey, the Indian wars of the 1860s and 1870s, the near extinction of the bison, and the starvation winter of 1883 and were living on the Blackfeet Reservation. They had no reason to aid this American in his quest to find the pass they had so long kept secret. A railroad through the plains and across the mountains near their reservation would bring even more non-Indian settlers to crowd them onto ever-shrinking plots of land.

Stevens was able to convince Coonsah, a Salish guide, to take him into the mountains. They didn't get far before they encountered snow piled so deep the horses could not get through.

Stevens would not give up. He and the reluctant Coonsah strung rawhide into snowshoes and began their journey across the brutally cold expanse. Several miles short of the pass, Coonsah announced he would go no farther, and Stevens continued alone. He had studied Greenhow's map, Tinkham's and Doty's reports, and the description of the pass the Blackfeet had given to Governor Isaac Stevens years before. By skill or by luck, he walked right into it, crossing the Continental Divide and dropping into the western drainage.

Convinced he had crossed the Divide and satisfied he had found the lowest pass across the Rocky Mountains, Stevens turned back. He camped at the crest of the Divide in bitter forty-below-zero temperatures. Elated that he had found the pass and utterly exhausted from the effort, he didn't dare lie down for fear of lapsing into a deep sleep and freezing, never to awake. He gathered wood, somehow got a fire started, and paced back and forth all night.

At daybreak he set out for the Blackfeet Agency at Badger Creek. On the way, he came across the nearly frozen Coonsah, whose fire had gone out during the night. Stevens revived him, and the two went on to the agency to report that he had found the secret pass across the mountains.

A monument of Stevens is located at the summit of the pass, which is now known as Marias Pass.

*Piikáni camp near
St. Mary Lakes.*
Circa 1890s.
Courtesy K. Ross Toole Archives,
University of Montana–Missoula.
94-1151.

A Great Native Nation Yields

For 140 years the South Piikáni tribe of the Niitsitapi (now known as the Blackfeet) had managed to hang on to their precarious dominance over the northern Great Plains and the mountains of Glacier. The end of their reign had been coming since the first traders entered their country in the 1820s. The 1870 Massacre on the Marias and the near extinction of the bison in the 1880s delivered the final blows.

Massacre on the Marias

One of the most horrific events to impact the Piikáni occurred in 1870, the result of events that began three years earlier.

Owl Child, the son of Mountain Chief, traveled to Helena, Montana, to visit his cousin Cutting Off Head Woman in 1867. She had married the former fur trader Malcolm Clarke, and they were living on his ranch.

During the visit, Owl Child's horses were stolen. He blamed Clarke and stole some of Clarke's horses, retreating to Mountain Chief's camp. Clarke and his son Horace tracked him to the camp and confronted him. Horace struck Owl Child, calling him a dog. Clarke called Owl Child an old woman. In the Piikáni culture these attacks on Owl Child's honor warranted

action. Two years later, in August 1869, Owl Child and twenty-four warriors rode to the ranch and killed Clarke and wounded Horace.

The citizens of Helena were outraged and swore out warrants for the arrest of Owl Child and his men. The U.S. marshal in Helena turned the warrants over to the superintendent of Indian Affairs for the U.S. Army, Gen. Alfred Sully. Sully took the warrants to the tribal chiefs. They agreed to turn Owl Child over but took no action. At the time, Owl Child and his group were traveling with Mountain Chief to his winter camp.

General Sheridan, who was in charge of the Military Division of the Missouri, ordered Lt. Col. E. M. Baker to make a surprise attack on Mountain Chief's winter camp and "strike them hard." On January 23, 1870, Lieutenant Colonel Baker, his scout Joe Kipp, and a column of cavalry and mounted infantry rode through a blinding blizzard during the night to what they thought was the winter camp of Mountain Chief near the Marias River. When Kipp saw the camp, he realized it was not that of Mountain Chief. He told Baker, but Baker

*A former fur trader
for the American Fur
Company, Malcolm
Clarke was killed
by Piikáni warriors,
which set off a series
of events that led to
the massacre of Chief
Heavy Runner and
other innocent Piikáni
in his village—and to
the end of the Piikáni
resistance.*
Circa 1850s.
Courtesy Overholser
Historical Research Center,
Fort Benton, Montana.

ordered Kipp shot if he tried to interfere and continued to deploy his dismounted troops in a skirmish line along the ridge above the camp. As dawn broke on the sleeping village, Baker's army attacked, firing blindly into the lodges.

The soldiers were firing on the smallpox-ridden camp of the peaceful Piikáni leader Heavy Runner. Heavy Runner ran out of his tepee waving his papers and his peace medal to stop the terrible slaughter but was shot down.

Baker's official report stated that 120 warriors had been killed and 53 women and children accidentally shot. Indian agent Lt. W. A. Pease was outraged by the report and made his own, stating that most of the camp's men had been away hunting, and only fifteen of the dead were fighting men. Ninety of the bodies were women and fifty were children, most suffering from smallpox. Fearing the disease, the soldiers burned the lodges and turned the 140 surviving women and children into the cold of winter to survive any way they could.

As John C. Jackson points out in *The Piikáni Blackfeet, a Culture Under Siege,* the Piikáni had suffered similar atrocities in the past and even inflicted them on other tribes. But this time, after years of losing their people to smallpox and their lands to the advancing nation of states, and the foreboding presence of the U.S. Army in their territory, the Piikáni, like the other Indians on the plains, no longer wanted war. The Piikáni resistance to American invasion along Montana's front range had ended.

The Near Extinction of the Bison

In the early nineteenth century, an estimated thirty million bison roamed throughout North America. Just eighty years later only a few hundred remained.

In 1840 the European demand for bison hides increased. The hide was used to make fashionable winter coats, lap robes, and rugs, as well as to make belts for industrial machines. The bison hide trade in the northern Great Plains soon surpassed the trade of beaver pelts.

Despite a rapid decline in bison population by the 1870s, several hundred hide hunters, including Indians who hunted both for their food and for hides for trading, were killing 2,000 to 100,000 bison a day depending on the season. Nearly six million bison hides were shipped to Europe between 1871 and 1883.

The disappearance of the bison threatened the Piikáni nomadic way of life, which had existed for thousands of years. Like most Plains Indians, they survived on bison meat and used the hides to make their tepees, winter coats, and moccasins. There was little the bison did not provide, and without them the free roaming ways of the Piikáni were lost.

In the summer of 1883 two Piikáni bands went to the Sweetgrass Hills to look for bison. They killed only six. That winter and the two winters that followed are known by the Piikáni as "the starvation winters." The bison had all but disappeared and the starving Piikáni were forced to move onto the reservations,

where conditions proved to be no better. Drought and early and late frosts destroyed the reservation crops, government supplies were delayed or inedible when they arrived, and cattle herds on the reservation were used to feed the starving Indians. Finally in 1885 Congress passed a special appropriation to address the deplorable conditions on the reservations. But for some it was too late; nearly one-quarter of the Piikáni population had died during the starvation winters of 1883 to 1885.

The memory of the 1870 massacre, the loss of the bison, and the suffering during the starvation winters brought the Piikáni traditional way of life to an end.

Whiskey Traders

It had been illegal to sell liquor in Indian country since the U.S. Congress passed the Trade and Intercourse Acts of 1822, 1832, and 1834 to regulate non-Indian commerce and travel in Indian country. The fur trade companies were the most affected by the law. They depended on commerce with the Indians, who brought hides and pelts to the trading posts in exchange for a variety of goods including guns and whiskey.

Despite federal law, whiskey traders were determined to continue to make and sell whiskey, and they found creative ways to do so.

Founders of Fort Whoop-up, Alfred B. Hamilton (above) and John J. Healy (below).
Circa 1880s.
Courtesy Overholser Historical Research Center, Fort Benton, Montana.

Healy, Hamilton, and Fort Whoop-up

In 1869 entrepreneurial scoundrels John J. Healy and his partner Alfred B. Hamilton obtained a permit from the Piikáni Indian agent to cross the Blackfeet Reservation into Canada. The permit stated they were not to trade with the Indians. Healy and Hamilton indicated they understood—knowing that once they crossed the border into Canada, the rules no longer applied. The Hudson Bay Company had only recently ceded these lands to Canada, and no liquor laws were yet in place.

The two traders, leading about thirty men with six wagons loaded with supplies, arrived at the winter camp of the Kainaa and Piikáni at the junction of the St. Mary and Belly rivers, some forty miles northeast of today's Glacier National Park. They quickly constructed a stockade cabin, named it Fort Hamilton, and began trading with the tribes, exchanging whiskey and rifles for bison hides and furs.

Fort Standoff, at the junction of the Belly and Waterton rivers, was named after an incident involving trader Joe Kipp, who bluffed a U.S. marshal out of taking him into custody.

Joe Kipp's Trading Post, C. M. Russell, 1898. Courtesy of Buffalo Bill Historical Center, Cody, Wyoming. Gift of Charles Ulrick and Josephine Bay Foundation, Inc.: 1.85.

The fort was better known as Fort Whoop-up, and business boomed. Six months after establishing the fort, Healy and Hamilton returned to Fort Benton with bison robes and furs worth nearly $50,000. Word of their success reached other traders, and soon "whiskey forts" were popping up on the southern Canadian plains.

Fort Slide-out was established near the border on the Belly River, and fur trader John Kennedy established a small whiskey post at the junction of the St. Mary River and Kennedy Creek, near the northeast corner of today's Glacier National Park.

Joe Kipp and Fort Standoff

In 1871 trader and scout Joe Kipp built Fort Standoff, named for an incident with the law, at the junction of the Belly and Waterton rivers.

Fervor for adventure seemed to run in Joe Kipp's

blood. Born in 1847, Joe was the son of Earth Woman, a Mandan, and James Kipp, an American Fur Company trader whose adventures in Montana were legendary. James Kipp had established Fort Union at the mouth of the Yellowstone River and Fort Piegan, the first trading post in Piikáni country, at the mouth of the Marias River.

Joe Kipp grew up at Fort Union and at Fort Benton, the hub of the fur trade in the Northwest. He spoke English, French, Piikáni, Sioux, Gros Ventre, Crow, Mandan, and Arikara. At Fort Benton he worked for the factor Andrew Dawson.

When the younger Kipp heard the news of the fur trading success at Fort Whoop-up across the U.S./Canada border, he convinced his old friend and prospecting partner Charles Thomas to join him and become a fur trader. They crossed the border and built a trading post in Canada.

According to Kipp, as chronicled by guide and author James Willard Schultz, while the U.S. marshal was in Fort Benton, Kipp slipped into Helena, Montana, and bought 750 gallons of alcohol. He loaded it onto rafts and paddled north on the Missouri River to the mouth of the Sun River. Thomas was waiting for him there with three four-horse teams and wagons, some teamsters, and a cook. After loading the alcohol, the party started north by way of the Indian and Red River cart trails, later known as the Sun River Trail.

Three days later, just after crossing the North Fork of the Milk River, they saw a lone horseman approaching. Realizing it must be U.S. Marshal Harding from Helena, Kipp said, "We may as well stop right here and stand him off."

Marshal Harding passed the first and second wagons and rode straight on to the third, which Kipp was driving. "Well, Joe, I've got you at last," he said. "Just turn around and head for Fort Benton."

"Harding, you are just twenty minutes too late," Kipp answered. "You should have overtaken on the far side of the creek back there."

"Oh, come. No joshing. This is serious business. Turn your team," Harding insisted.

"Harding, right here you are no more a marshal of the United States than I am, for here we are in Canada; the North Fork of the Milk River is the line," Kipp said.

In fact, the international boundary had not yet been surveyed and marked; however, it was generally believed that Chief Mountain and the North Fork of the Milk River were on or very close to the forty-ninth parallel, which designated the U.S./Canada border.

After some quick thinking, Harding replied. "You have no proof that we are in Canada. I'll take chances that we are south of the line. I arrest you all for having liquor in your possession in Indian country. Turn your outfit around and we'll strike out for Fort Benton."

Kipp laughed. "Marshal, you have no proof that we are not north of the line. Anyhow, we'll take the chance that we're in Canada and we are five against you—five to one. Right here we stand you off."

After a few more threats, Harding suddenly wheeled his horse around and galloped away.

Kipp and his men drove to their post on the Belly River and christened it Fort Standoff to commemorate their encounter with the U.S. marshal.

Squelching the Whiskey Trade

Whiskey increased the violence between Indians and settlers and had disastrous effects on the tribes of the Northwest. Drunken quarrels and fights among the Siksiká, Kainaa, and Piikáni ended in death to many and nearly destroyed their culture. Canada responded in 1873 by expediting the formation of the Northwest Mounted Police at the border. A year later the red-uniformed Mounties brought law to western Canada and squelched the whiskey trade.

Miners

The remarkable mountains of today's Glacier National Park were not spared from the grip of gold fever or the search for oil. It started with a trickle of prospectors—some just passing through on their way to Canada, and others who are said to have found a gold nugget here and there but left for more promising fields in California. The real mining boom came during the last half of the 1880s.

Trading on the Frontier

On the frontier, trading was often on credit. An Indian who came to a fort was given a gun, powder, shot, and other "necessaries," which he swore to pay for with beaver pelts, also known as "plus" (pronounced *plews*), from his winter trapping.

2 plus = 1 small item such as an ax, kettle, beaver trap, or length of cloth
6 plus = 1 blanket
14 plus = 1 gun
30 plus = 1 keg of whiskey

A motley bunch of whiskey traders. Left to right, Mose Solomon, Joe Kipp, Bob Mills, Henry Kennerly, and John Largent.
Circa 1870s.
Courtesy Overholser
Historical Research Center,
Fort Benton, Montana.

E.R. Shepard, circa 1890s.
Courtesy Montana Historical Society, Helena, Montana.

Elizabeth "Libby" (Smith) Collins

The best known of Glacier's mining speculators was Elizabeth Collins—later immortalized as the Cattle Queen of Montana in the 1954 film of the same name starring Barbara Stanwyck and Ronald Reagan. Known as Auntie Collins or Libby Collins, Elizabeth was married to cattle rancher Nathaniel Collins of Choteau, Montana.

Collins' mining venture began when her brother located a quartz vein while prospecting on upper Mineral Creek. She took on a partner, Frank McPartland, and persuaded some investors from St. Paul, Minnesota, to finance the operation. They hired eighteen men to remove the copper from the mine, which was located along present-day Cattle Queen Creek. The crew worked for three summers and one winter, but the mine did not produce much and was eventually abandoned.

After the failure of the mine, the Cattle Queen went back to ranching. After a couple of years, gold fever drove her to the Klondike to again seek her fortune. Eventually she returned to Choteau, where she dutifully cared for her sick husband until his death. She then sold the ranch and moved to California.

Dutch Louis Meyer had been prospecting in the mountains west of the Continental Divide for four years when he finally uncovered a vein of gold, silver, copper, and lead-carrying quartz on the Divide at the head of Copper (Valentine) Creek in 1889. It didn't take long for the news to spread to the mining towns of Butte, Helena, and Anaconda. Three hundred miners shouldered their picks and headed north. In a frenzy to seek their wealth, they staked 2,000 placer and lode mining claims throughout the glaciated mountains west of the Continental Divide. The claims turned out to be of little value and were soon abandoned.

Three years later oil seepages were discovered near Kintla Lake, setting off a small oil boom. Speculators filed oil and mineral claims and constructed crude shacks, a road, and Montana's first oil rig. Kintla's oil boom lasted for about a year and then was abandoned because removing the small amount of oil was too expensive.

In 1895 the Piikáni agreed to sell their land east of the Continental Divide, in what is now Glacier National Park. At noon on April 15, 1898, a musket boomed, declaring the area open for prospecting. Libby Collins and fewer than 100 miners braved ten feet of snow to stake claims.

Miners staked claims on Roes Creek, Boulder Creek, and Otatso Creek, but the most notable strikes were at Cracker Lake, near present-day Many Glacier in the Swiftcurrent Valley. A wild, rip-roaring boomtown practically sprang up overnight near Swiftcurrent Falls in the flats

The wild mining boom-town of Altyn, near Many Glacier.
1904. Courtesy Glacier National Park Archives.

below where the Many Glacier Hotel now stands. Stores, a post office, several saloons, a hotel, and cabins were hastily built. The new town was christened Altyn in honor of Dave Greenwood Altyn, one of the financial backers of the Cracker Lake Mine.

By 1902 the investors and toiling miners grew fed up with the meager treasures this rugged country offered for their brutally hard labor. They packed up their shovels and picks and headed for the Klondike, and Altyn faded into a ghost town.

Gallery of Early Glacier Guides

About the same time miners were combing the mountains for minerals, prominent Easterners—some with a passion for hunting and fishing and others with interests in science and exploration—became interested in the rugged land that is now Glacier National Park. Many are well-known figures in American history: conservationist George Bird Grinnell, English banker Cecil Baring, publisher Ralph Pulitzer, and Henry L. Stimson, who later became U.S. secretary of state and was twice secretary of war. All these men needed guides to take them through the rugged land that captured their imaginations.

The first generation of guides in what is now Glacier National Park comprised former fur trappers

Miners use a sluice ramp to search for gold.
Courtesy Glacier National Park Archives.

or their sons. They had honed their skills living as mountain men and later scouting for the U.S. Army. They knew the country and the Indians and could speak the Piikáni language. These men carried a ready weapon and were good shots. They knew where game could be found, and their camps always had a good supply of meat and fish. Many of their names are lost to history, but a few remain embedded in Glacier National Park history, including Hugh Monroe's grandson William (Billy) Jackson, Joe Kipp, and Tom Dawson.

William Jackson

William "Billy" Jackson was the grandson of fur trapper and mountain man Hugh Monroe, presumably the first non-Indian to explore what is now Glacier National Park. As early as age eight, Billy Jackson was traveling with his grandfather trapping furs in the Two Medicine Valley. By the time he was in his teens, he was a skilled trapper and woodsman.

In 1873, when Jackson was seventeen, he and his older brother Robert enlisted as Army scouts for Col. George Armstrong Custer and the Seventh Cavalry. At the time, Custer and the Seventh were escorting Northern Pacific Railway route surveyors from Bismarck, North Dakota, across the plains to the Yellowstone River.

Jackson scouted for Custer for the next three years. To his good fortune, he was assigned to Maj. Marcus Reno's troop, narrowly avoiding death at the Battle of the Little Bighorn in 1876. According to his account of the battle, just as the Sioux were about to outflank Custer's men, Major Reno waved his gun, shouted something Billy couldn't hear, and rode back across the river to a bluff in order to make a stand. On the run to the bluff, Billy and another scout were cut off by several Sioux; they ducked into a stand of timber to avoid being seen. Riding low, under fire from the Sioux, they disappeared into the thick brush and followed a trail up a slope, finally coming onto Captain Benteen's company—but by then the fighting at the Little Bighorn was over.

Billy Jackson and his brother scouted for the Army under Col. Nelson Miles for another year. Then he quit the Army and joined his family, who were living among a band of Piikáni near the Bears Paw and Little Rocky mountains. It was here that Jackson met James

William Jackson poses in buckskin, looking every bit the frontiersman.
Circa 1900.
Courtesy Beinecke Rare Book and Manuscript Library, Yale University.

Willard Schultz and Joe Kipp. Jackson and Schultz became fast friends. Schultz started a guide and outfitter business in Glacier and hired Billy as his guide.

In the years that followed, Billy guided Gifford Pinchot, the first chief of the Forest Service, and a government commission on an inspection tour through the Glacier area to form a policy for national forests. He guided George Bird Grinnell and the writer Emerson Hough when they investigated the lands of the "ceded strip," and he and Joe Kipp were present during the1895 land negotiations with the Piikáni.

Jackson married, had four children, and ranched in the Cut Bank area. He died from a sudden illness in 1902. Jackson Glacier and Mount Jackson are named for him.

Joe Kipp

The most famous guide in the Glacier area was Joe Kipp. Kipp was the son of James Kipp, the legendary American Fur Company trader, and Earth Woman, the granddaughter of the Mandan Chief Mato-tope (Four Bears), whose portrait was painted by artist George Catlin in 1833 and Swiss artist Karl Bodmer in 1834 during their visits to the Mandan village.

Kipp had an abundance of grit and the confidence to try his hand at just about anything: prospecting, scouting for the Army, whiskey trading, cattle ranching, and guiding. He is frequently mentioned throughout the early history of the park.

In 1870 Kipp was the U.S. Army scout who warned Lt. Col. E. M. Baker just before the infamous Massacre on the Marias that the troops were attacking the wrong village.

It was Kipp who built Fort Standoff across the Canadian border and traded whiskey to the Piikáni for beaver pelts and bison hides. When the Canadian Mounties put a stop to that lucrative business, he used his bull train to freight goods from Fort Benton to various mountain towns.

Joe Kipp.
Circa 1870s.
Courtesy Overholser Historical
Research Center,
Fort Benton, Montana.

Kipp also prospected for minerals around Flattop Mountain. He tried his hand at raising cattle and then returned to fur trading. In 1878 he bought Fort Conrad on the Marias River and hired the young adventurer and chronicler James Willard Schultz to work for him. In 1886 Kipp sold the fort and turned to guiding for adventurous gentlemen from the East who came to hunt and fish or explore the rugged mountains.

Schultz wrote that Kipp taught him the ways of the frontier; he immortalized Kipp in the 1907 book *My Life as an Indian*.

Kipp married Chief Heavy Runner's daughter Double Strike Woman in 1877. They had three children, Mary, James, and George, and adopted the children of Double Strike Woman's dead sister, William and Margaret Fitzgerald. In later years Kipp lived on his ranch near the town of Blackfoot, Montana.

Kipp Creek and Mount Kipp are named for the legendary guide.

Tom Dawson

Thomas Erskin Dawson—the son of Andrew Dawson, the chief fur trader for Chouteau and Company, and his Gros Ventre wife, Pipe Woman—was born in 1859 at Fort Benton, Montana. The elder Dawson wanted his son to attend London's Oxford University in preparation for the Foreign Service. At age thirteen Tom went off to Eaton for a year, but the family ran out of money for his education. For the next several years, Tom tried a variety of trades. He worked in a shipyard, joined the Northwest Mounties, became a logger, and then worked for Joe Kipp as a maintenance man at the Blackfeet Indian Agency. While he was working for Kipp, he met fur trader Malcolm Clarke's daughter Isabel. They married in 1891, and the couple worked and lived at the Agency until 1893.

Isabel's brother Horace, who had survived Owl Child's 1869 attack that eventually led to the Massacre on the Marias, had, in 1888, moved onto land that would eventually border the Great Northern Railway on the north. In 1893 Tom and Isabel did the same thing, choosing land on the south side of the right of way. They built a ranch house about a mile west of the center of what is now the community of East Glacier and became ranchers; Tom also worked as a guide.

Tom pioneered trails in the Two Medicine Valley, guiding hunting parties until 1910, when the area became a national park. He was guide for railroad barons James and Louis Hill, as well as explorer Dr. Lyman Sperry, and he worked as an interpreter for writer Mary Roberts Rinehart.

Dawson's wanderlust was satisfied. He spent the remaining years of his life on his ranch. He died in 1953 at age ninety-four and was buried in the Clarke-Dawson Cemetery near East Glacier.

Dawson Pass is named for Tom Dawson. Isabel

Lake is named after his wife, Isabel Dawson.

Early Chroniclers

Until the 1870s, when the Indian wars on the plains ended, the human drama and natural wonders in what is now Glacier National Park had passed relatively unnoticed by the Eastern press.

During the preceding forty years, journalists, historians, artists, and photographers generally reported from where the great sagas of the West were unfolding at the time: the mass immigrations and settlement in Oregon and Utah, the wars between the immigrants and the Southwest tribes in Arizona and New Mexico, and the rush for silver and gold in California, Nevada, and Colorado. They reported facts as well as created legends to satisfy readers enthralled with the American West.

When writers finally ventured into the northern Rockies in the 1870s, they sparked a nation's enduring love affair with the beauty and history of the glaciated mountains and the Indian tribes that called them home.

Tom Dawson.
1914.
Courtesy John Chase.

James Willard Schultz

The first of the Western adventure writers to gain national attention was James Willard Schultz.

Schultz had loved the outdoors since his childhood days camping and hunting in the mountains of the East. In 1877, at the age of eighteen, he left New York for the mountains of the Northwest. He quickly took up with mountain men Hugh Monroe and Joe Kipp and became friends with Tail Feathers Coming-over-the-Hill and other Piikáni. He learned their language, lived as they lived, and joined them on hunts. The Piikáni gave him the name Apikuni, meaning Spotted Robe, and at age twenty he married the Piikáni woman Fine Shield.

Schultz soon began writing about his adventures in the Rocky Mountains. His first stories were printed in the sports magazine *Forest and Stream.* In 1907 he wrote his first book, *My Life as an Indian,* and in 1916 his *Blackfeet Tales of Glacier National Park* was published.

His stories of life among the Indians thrilled readers and introduced the world to the magnificence of Glacier and the Blackfeet culture.

Many of today's place names in Glacier National

Mountain man and author James Willard Schultz. He learned the ways of the Piikáni while living with the tribe and listening to the tales of Hugh Monroe and Joe Kipp.
Circa 1880s.
Courtesy Overholser Historical Research Center,
Fort Benton, Montana.

Park were chosen by Schultz, including Goat Mountain, Glacier Wall, Going-to-the-Sun Mountain, Heavy Runner Peak, and Singleshot Mountain.

By the end of Schultz's life, he had written thirty-seven books, twenty-seven of which were serialized in magazines such as *Youth's Companion* and *American Boy,* popular children's publications from 1912 through 1932. Schultz died in 1947 as one of the foremost non-Indian writers of Blackfeet stories.

George Bird Grinnell

Of the many articles James Willard Schultz submitted to *Forest and Stream,* none had more impact than the story that landed on the desk of editor George Bird Grinnell in 1885. Titled *To the Chief Mountain,* the article described hunting bighorn sheep and mountain goats and catching twelve-pound trout in lakes "walled in by stupendous mountains…peak after peak of jagged mountains, sheer cliffs thousands of feet high and a true glacier . . . at least 300 feet thick."

Brooklyn born and Yale educated, George Bird Grinnell was an ardent naturalist, adventurer, and big-game hunter. In 1874 he accompanied Professor Othniel C. Marsh of the Peabody Museum on a fossil-collecting expedition to the western territories. Col. George Custer escorted the expedition through the Black Hills of South Dakota. Two years later he accompanied Col. William Ludlow in his 1876 fossil-collecting expedition through what is now Yellowstone National Park.

Grinnell was so captivated by Schultz's article that he immediately left New York on a train for Helena, Montana, then took a mail stage to Fort Benton to meet Schultz. The two traveled to the Glacier area by wagon and then set out on horseback to explore and hunt game in the mountains.

While hunting on the mountain next to East Flattop during a snowstorm, Grinnell brought down a bighorn sheep with a single shot. The event prompted Schultz to give the name Singleshot to the uniquely shaped mountain. Later, Grinnell, Schultz, and their Piikáni guide Otokomi took a two-day trip through a river valley to reach a glacier they had seen from afar. Grinnell gave the name Swiftcurrent to the valley and river, and the glacier they explored would later be named for him. The naming of the Garden Wall and

George Bird Grinnell and his wife, Elizabeth Grinnell, on Grinnell Glacier. The glacier was named for him in 1887.
Courtesy Glacier National Park Archives.

Gunsight Pass are also attributed to Grinnell.

This eventful hunting trip was the beginning of Grinnell's fascination with Glacier and his long campaign to preserve it. He returned annually for many years and wrote numerous vividly descriptive articles proclaiming the magnificence of Glacier, in which he coined the phrase "Crown of the Continent," which is still used today to refer to the park and its rare beauty.

In 1907 he convinced Montana Senator Thomas Carter to introduce a bill establishing a national park to protect the area. Grinnell worked tirelessly until the bill passed in 1910 after three failed attempts.

In addition to helping create Glacier National Park, Grinnell was one of the founders of the Audubon Society and, together with President Theodore Roosevelt, founded the Boone and Crockett Club. In 1925 he received the Theodore Roosevelt Distinguished Service Medal for his work to preserve Yellowstone and Glacier national parks. Grinnell died in 1938 at the age of eighty-nine.

Walter McClintock

Glacier National Park's McClintock Peak is named after adventurer and writer Walter McClintock. In 1896, five years after he graduated from Yale, the twenty-six-year-old headed west, working as a photographer for Gifford Pinchot's U.S. Forest Service expedition to examine the resources of the national forests.

McClintock befriended the scout William "Billy" Jackson and spent four years living with the Piikáni.

Piikáni medicine man Brings Down the Sun relates Blackfeet stories to adventurer and author Walter McClintock.
Circa 1900.
Courtesy Beinecke Rare Book and Manuscript Library, Yale University.

McClintock kept detailed records of his experiences with the tribe, from daily life to hunts to rituals and ceremonies. He took some 2,000 photographs, which he used to illustrate his account of life among the area's Indians in the 1910 book *The Old North Trail: Life, Legends, and Religion of the Blackfeet Indians.*

In addition to *The Old North Trail*, he authored *Old Indian Trails, The Tragedy of the Blackfoot, Blackfoot Culture, The Warrior Societies,* and *Swan Song of the Red Warrior.*

Over Valley, Plain, and Peak

The Glacier area would see its biggest push for development and settlement when railroad baron James J. Hill began building the Great Northern Railway from the Great Lakes to the Pacific Ocean.

The Empire Builder

Known as the Empire Builder, James J. Hill and his transcontinental railroad lured thousands of immigrants to the Dakotas and Montana to farm the prairies and plains and build cities. He became the most prolific railroad baron in history and eventually controlled nearly a quarter of the railroads in the western United States.

Hill's career as a railroad baron began in 1878, when he bought the financially crippled St. Paul and Pacific Railway for about twenty percent of its value. A year later he laid track and began running trains from St. Paul, Minnesota, to Winnipeg, Canada. Then Hill set out to achieve his greatest ambition: to build the United States' fifth transcontinental railway. By 1889 he had the rails of his transcontinental Great Northern Railway laid from St. Paul to the base of the Rocky Mountains.

Determined to find the easiest pass across the Rocky Mountains, Hill sent location engineer John F. Stevens to locate a pass known only to Indians and perhaps a few trappers. In 1889 Stevens found the pass, and by 1891 the rails had been laid and trains were rolling through Marias Pass and along the Middle Fork of the Flathead River, bordering the breathtaking scenery of what would become Glacier National Park, and on to Columbia Falls, Kalispell, and points west. Meanwhile track for the Great Northern Railway was being laid from Seattle eastward to connect with the rails being laid westward. The rails from east

James J. Hill, the most successful railroad baron in U.S. history. He constructed the most financially sound transcontinental railroad in the nation, facilitated the population of the Northwest, and reigned over a quarter of all the railroads in the West.
Circa 1912.
Courtesy Minnesota Historical Society and Burlington Northern–Santa Fe Railway.

Newspaper cartoon of Hill planning his railway lines.
Courtesy Minnesota Historical Society.

to west were connected in the Cascade Mountains on January 6, 1893.

The Whistle Call

Once the rails were laid, crews began building water towers, coal storage bins, and roundhouses for helper engines on either side of the steep grades through the mountains. At one time, there were as many as eleven water and coal stops and railroad yards or stations along the sixty-mile route following the Middle Fork of the Flathead River. Settlements to house and feed the men who tended the roundhouses, water towers, and coal chutes quickly grew up around Midvale (East Glacier), Summit, Bear Creek (Blacktail), Java, Essex, Nyack, and Belton (West Glacier).

But this was just a glimpse of the future. When Hill completed his transcontinental railroad in 1893,

Driving the last spike on the Great Northern Railway in the Cascade Mountains on January 6, 1893.
Courtesy Minnesota Historical Society and Burlington Northern–Santa Fe Railway.

the pounding of the final spike was like a whistle call to Easterners. His station agents had already begun creating magnificent advertising brochures to entice settlers to the Northwest and tourists to Lake McDonald.

Living on the Edge of a Wilderness

When the Great Northern Railway work train moved down the line toward Kalispell in 1891, the railroad left two small boxcars to serve as the Belton Station. It would be a regular stop for trains running east and west. It also brought the first permanent families to the area that is now Glacier National Park.

Belton in its heyday in 1914. A more modern Belton Station, at the far right, replaced two boxcars that once served as the train station. The path at the lower right leads to the Belton Chalet.
Ted Marble, 1914.
Courtesy Glacier National Park Archives.

Great Northern Railway stationery advertising Apgar's Summer Resort at Lake McDonald. 1906.
Courtesy Glacier National Park Archives.

Frontier bachelors Bill Daucks, Frank Geduhn, Esli Apgar, and Dimon Apgar pose under a WIVES WANTED sign tacked to a cabin at Apgar. Their solemn faces say it all.
Circa 1901.
Courtesy Glacier National Park Archives.

By 1893 Charlie Howes, Milo Apgar, and Frank Geduhn had built homes at the foot of Lake McDonald. A short time later Frank Geduhn moved to the head of the lake, and Denis Comeau, Frank Kelly, and George Snyder also built cabins there.

While these hearty settlers enjoyed the fishing, hunting, and scenery of Glacier—some working in the Flathead Valley to earn money to maintain their homesteads—the Great Northern Railway was distributing eloquent publicity booklets in the East that touted beautiful Lake McDonald as a tourist site. At the same time, George Bird Grinnell's articles in *The Century* and *Forest and Stream* magazines were piquing the interest of Eastern tourists, who were traveling to the West in ever-increasing numbers.

Belton became a busy railroad stop, and soon a small town grew up around it. Edward Dow built a two-story hotel, a saloon, and a store and post office. Milo Apgar and other settlers built rental cabins at the foot of Lake McDonald, establishing the small village known as Apgar. George Snyder settled near the head of the lake and built a hotel that would later become the site of today's Lake McDonald Lodge.

Tourists who wanted to spend an evening in George Snyder's hotel were taken around the lake on horseback over a trail; in 1895 Snyder purchased a forty-foot steamboat to ferry tourists from Apgar to his hotel.

By the turn of the twentieth century, settlers were cutting trails through the woods, operating boats on the lake, building more cabins and hotels, running stage lines, and generally prospering in the glow of the nation's newest and most glorious vacation spot.

II. Glacier National Park

Glaciers like this one lured explorers and naturalists to the area—and gave the park its name. Naturalist and conservationist George Bird Grinnell surveys the remarkable scenery from the glacier named for him.
Courtesy Montana Historical Society, Helena, Montana.

5

Prelude to a Park
1900–1909

T HE 1800S HAD BEEN A TIME OF RAPID CHANGE *for the nation. By 1900 the great western wildernesses had been explored, mapped, and partially settled. The Union had grown from sixteen states to forty-five. Nearly seventy-six million people occupied the United States, five transcontinental railroads stretched from coast to coast, and the fledgling nation had become the world's largest industrial power. The turn of the twentieth century brought more landmark events:*

President William McKinley was assassinated, and the cowboy Vice President Theodore Roosevelt took the oath of office in 1901. San Francisco rose from the ashes of the 1906 earthquake. Henry Ford introduced the Model T, Orville and Wilbur Wright launched the era of mechanized flight, and the telephone came into widespread use.

Amid the prosperity, renowned naturalist John Muir warned that "Thousands of tired, nerve-shaken, over-civilized people are beginning to find out that… wilderness is a necessity." He was right. The trickle of conservation initiatives begun in the last half of the 1800s turned into a flood in the early 1900s. The public was gripped with enthusiasm for the outdoors, and the voices of conservationists echoed in the halls of the U.S. Congress.

These changing attitudes set the stage for a series of events that ultimately led to the creation of Glacier National Park.

The Ceded Strip

"My eyes were long ago opened to the purposes of the Government. No other reservation has as valuable land as that which you come to buy," said White Calf, the war-weary leader of the Piikáni to the U.S. commissioners sent in 1895 to negotiate the purchase of what would one day become the eastern half of Glacier, including some land south of the park.

White Calf, the warrior Big Nose, and thirty-three other Piikáni (Blackfeet) leaders faced William C. Pollock of the Bureau of Indian Affairs, George Bird Grinnell, and Georgia attorney Walter M. Clements, who were there to negotiate the sale of the Blackfeet Reservation land from the reservation's western border at the Continental Divide to Birch Creek along the front range of the Rocky Mountains.

Since 1870 there had been a steady clamor from miners and homesteaders to open up this land for public use. The Great Northern Railway had laid track

Eight of the thirty-five Piikáni (Blackfeet) leaders who negotiated the sale of the "ceded strip," a portion of the original Blackfeet Reservation that is now the eastern half of Glacier National Park. According to the tribe, this is one of the most important photographs in their history. It features most of the tribe's leaders together, shortly after they settled on the reservation. Left to right are Running Crane, White Grass, Four Horns, Brocky (formally Tail Feathers Coming-over-the-Hill), White Calf, Bear Chief, and Little Plume, with Little Dog seated in the front, center. Big Nose (formally Three Suns) is not pictured.

J. N. Choate, 1895.
Courtesy National Anthropological
Archives, Smithsonian Institution.

through the reservation and along the southern border of what would one day become Glacier National Park. Great Northern Railway agents had begun to realize the potential of the glaciated landscape just north of the railroad for attracting passengers. The powerful influence of the railroad combined with that of miners and homesteaders spawned a movement to reduce the size of the Blackfeet Reservation and make the land available to the American public.

The Blackfeet had been struggling to protect their borders from outsiders for years. Now, largley dependent on government subsidy, they had neither the numbers nor the political power to defend their territory from these new powerful pressures. Acting Indian agent Capt. Lorenzo W. Cooke told the Blackfeet leaders that the best way to be rid of their problem with trespassers was to sell the land.

During the council the normally conciliatory White Calf asked $3 million for the land. Big Nose, who had always taken a position of keeping their lands, reversed his position and announced, "We are to sell some land that is of little use to us . . . If you wish to give a good price we will be pleased." After a few more days of talk, the Piikáni leaders accepted $1.5 million for the land.

Eight months later, on June 10, 1896, Congress ratified the treaty to re-draw the boundaries of the Blackfeet Reservation. Fourteen years later this "ceded strip" would become the eastern part of Glacier National Park.

Whispers of Preservation

Americans have been vigorous consumers of timber since the first colonists arrived. They cut down trees to build houses, cleared fields for crops, chopped firewood for cooking and heat, and quickly learned to exploit the great forests of the continent for profit.

By the 1700s Americans were shipping lumber to Europe and throughout the world. In the 1860s, when the first transcontinental railroads were being built, the lumber trade boomed. The logging industry moved from forest to forest, leaving a graveyard of stumps in its wake.

As the nation was gobbling up its forests, it reluctantly began to recognize the importance of preserving some natural resources for the future. Congress established Yellowstone National Park—the first national

Early forest rangers. Third from the left is Albert "Death on the Trail" Reynolds, who later became a Glacier National Park ranger. On the far right is Frank Liebig, considered the first forest ranger in what is now Glacier National Park.
Courtesy Glacier National Park Archives.

park in the world—in 1872, followed by Yosemite and Sequoia national parks eighteen years later. In 1891 Congress established the first "forest reserves" to protect watersheds from erosion and flooding and to preserve the nation's timber supply from over harvesting. Six years later, in 1897, President Grover Cleveland issued proclamations establishing the Flathead and Lewis and Clark forest reserves in northern Montana. The Flathead Forest Reserve included the land that later would become Glacier National Park.

The First Forest Rangers

In the early days of the forest reserves, the rangers were known as "forest range riders." They were saloon keepers, ranchers, waiters, blacksmiths, Indian scouts, and cowboys who kept their day jobs and moonlighted as range riders. Jack Reuter, a settler at Belton, and C. F. Van Allen at Essex both had brief appointments in 1901. Frank Liebig is considered the first official forest ranger in Glacier. But before Reuter, Van Allen, and Liebig, there was the colorful Fred Herrig.

Herrig was a wrangler and hunting guide for Theodore Roosevelt in the badlands of North Dakota and later was one of Roosevelt's Rough Riders during the Spanish-American War. When the war was over, Herrig returned to Montana. He was trying to decide what new adventure to tackle when he heard the government was looking for range riders. Herrig, not one to go the long way when a shortcut would do, wrote to Theodore Roosevelt, then governor of New York, and asked for a job recommendation.

Roosevelt sent a personal note to U.S. Senator Thomas Carter of Montana recommending Herrig for the job, and he was hired.

A colorful adventurer, Herrig was an imposing figure, described by fellow adventurer Frank Liebig as "a big man, not extra tall, but broad, with powerful shoulders. He generally rode a dark bay horse, decked up with a silver-studded bridle and martingale. He wore mostly high-top boots, a big 44 strapped on his belt and he carried a 45-70 rifle in a scabbard on his saddle. He wore the rangers badge in plain sight, and Bruno, a big Russian wolfhound, was his steady companion."

In 1902 the range riders were renamed "forest rangers," and in addition to enforcing the laws, fighting fires, and keeping trails open, they were charged with surveying, estimating, and scaling timber—and know a few things about forestry and the livestock business.

When Flathead Forest Reserve supervisor F. N. Haines went looking for a man to fit the description, he discovered it was no easy task. Fate and Fred Herrig came to his rescue. Herrig said such a man lived at the foot of Lake McDonald: Frank Liebig.

Liebig came to Glacier in 1900, just as the mining booms reached their pitiful peak before being abandoned and replaced by a ho-hum oil boom near

At the request of Theodore Roosevelt, then governor of New York, legendary forest ranger Fred Herrig was hired to patrol the Upper North Fork of the Flathead Forest Reserve, the area bordering what is now Glacier National Park.
Courtesy Glacier National Park Archives.

Kintla. He built a cabin on the north shore of Lake McDonald and worked staking claims and writing up the paperwork for oil investors for $50 a month. He quickly grew tired of this work and took up oil claims of his own on the Belly River.

In a letter to Liebig, Haines wrote, "I'm looking for a good man to work as a ranger for Uncle Sam. I've heard a lot about you, Mr. Liebig. I heard you don't drink or get on a spree but the main thing is you know this country and are not afraid of anything." He continued, "Would you like to tackle the job? It pays sixty a month. You board yourself and furnish your own horses."

Liebig accepted the job and took the train from Belton to Kalispell to be sworn in. Haines handed him a notebook, a silver badge, a double-bitted ax, a one-man crosscut saw, a box of ammunition for his 45-70 rifle, and two big sheets of paper on which he was to write what he did each day to send in at the end of the month. "The whole country is yours, from Belton to Canada and across the Rockies to the prairie between Waterton Lake and the foot of St. Mary Lake," Haines told him. "You're to look for fires, timber thieves, squatters, and game violators. *Go to it and good luck.*"

Liebig did just that. He built a cabin at the head of Lake McDonald, flew the flag of the U.S. Bureau of Forestry from the rooftop, and began his job as the first official forest ranger patrolling a half million acres in the area now known as Glacier National Park.

Crusade to Create a Park

For the growing number of naturalists concerned with the area, the protections guaranteed under forest reserve designation were not enough. Mining, settlement, and other forms of development were allowed in forest reserves. The only designation that would adequately protect this unique piece of the American landscape was that of national park.

The first person to pursue this plan was U.S. Army Lt. John T. Van Orsdale, who sent a letter to the *Fort Benton River Press* in 1883 suggesting that "publicity now being given to that portion of Montana will result in drawing attention to the scenery which surpasses anything in Montana or adjacent territories. A great benefit would result to Montana if this section could be set aside as a national park."

When George Bird Grinnell began visiting the area

Louis W. Hill genuinely loved the area's mountains and valleys, but he also knew what national park status would bring to his business, the Great Northern Railway. He was a powerful voice among the movers and shakers in Washington, D.C., and one of the leaders promoting the bill to create Glacier National Park.
Courtesy Minnesota Historical Society and Burlington Northern–Santa Fe Railway. MHS Portrait Collection CN4.

Author and naturalist George Bird Grinnell, who coined the park's nickname Crown of the Continent, brought Glacier to national attention and used his magazine articles to promote the legislation that would eventually lead to the creation of Glacier National Park.
1920. Courtesy K. Ross Toole Archives, University of Montana (81.0295).

in 1885, he took up the cause, coining the term Crown of the Continent and bringing national attention to the notion of creating another national park. Grinnell enlisted the help of other frequent visitors to the glaciated mountains: noted author Emerson Hough, college professor and lecturer Dr. Lyman Sperry, and attorney L. O. Vaught.

Among the voices thundering to preserve the wilderness was Theodore Roosevelt. "I hate the man who would skin the land!" roared Teddy, and when he became president in 1901, he set out to save as much land as he could from timber barons, miners, cattle kings, and dam builders.

The long campaign to make the area a national park had garnered enough support by 1907 to get the attention of the U.S. Congress. U.S. Senator Thomas Carter of Montana introduced a bill to the Senate on December 11. It failed. Carter revised it and again presented it to the Senate in 1908. It was passed by the Senate and sent to the House of Representatives on May 16, where hard-working Congressman Charles N. Pray, Montana's only member of the House, ushered the bill through the Committee on Public Lands.

The committee recommended approval, but no action was taken and the bill died.

A determined Senator Carter introduced the bill to the Senate for the third time on June 26, 1909. This time it sat dormant in the Public Lands committee until January 15, 1910. While the bill languished in committee, Louis W. Hill, president of the Great Northern Railway, and other notables urged Congress to pass the bill.

Unfortunately, the first decade of the twentieth century came to a close without a decision on this hard-fought-for national park.

Congressman Charles N. Pray took advantage of a sweltering afternoon in Washington, D.C., with no air-conditioning in the Capitol, to call up the bill to create Glacier National Park. Most of the bill's opponents were absent due to the heat, and it was passed "before the bill's enemies knew what had happened."
Circa 1900.
Courtesy Overholser Historical Research Center, Fort Benton, Montana.

Montana's most famous artist, Charles M. Russell built Bull Head Lodge at the foot of the lake in 1906. He called it Bull Head Lodge after the bison skull next to the door; this bison skull became part of his signature on all his paintings. Charlie spent many summers in Glacier, telling yarns around the fireplace at Lewis' Hotel with friends James Willard Schultz, Joe Kipp, Mary Roberts Rinehart, Frank Linderman, Will Rogers, John Lewis, and other visitors to Glacier who happened by.
C. M. Russell, 1906.
Buffalo Bill Historical Center, Cody, Wyoming: 90.60.

Charles and Nancy Russell in front of Bull Head Lodge on Lake McDonald.
Circa 1906.
Courtesy C. M. Russell Museum, Great Falls, Montana.

Postcard of Glacier Park Lodge interior.
Courtesy Tom Mulvaney

Dazzling First Decade as a National Park
1910–1919

O N MAY 11, 1910, *President William Howard Taft signed the bill creating Glacier National Park. It had been a long road, but the park's advocates had prevailed in securing protection for the unique glaciated wilderness. Glacier's first decade as a national park saw a dizzying flurry of activity—as did the rest of the nation and the world. Outside park borders, Americans were embracing Hollywood, ragtime, and razzle-dazzle, and the women's suffrage movement was in full swing. World War I took our boys "over there," and a worldwide flu epidemic raged.*

Inside the borders, major park development was underway. A colorful crew of park rangers replaced the original forest rangers. The first automobiles rolled in, and roads, trails, hotels, and chalets appeared on Glacier's landscape. Saddle horses and stagecoaches, buses and boats carried sightseeing visitors from one grand locale to another. The segment of road that connected Belton to Apgar and later the Going-to-the-Sun Road was constructed, and Congress established the National Park Service to oversee the development and maintenance of all national parks.

The Big Blowup

The decade started with what Northwesterners called the Big Blowup. In July 1910 a rash of wildfires erupted throughout the Northwest, from Washington to Minnesota. In Idaho and Montana fires blackened more than 3 million acres, swallowing the towns of

Wallace and Mullan in Idaho, and Taft, Haugan, and Deborgia in Montana, and taking the lives of seventy-eight firefighters and seven others. The fires were still running rampant in August, forcing President William Howard Taft to authorize the Forest Service to hire additional men and to order the War Department to send in troops to help fight the fires.

The inferno spread throughout Glacier National Park. Dry lightning ignited wildfires from below Kintla Lake to the Canadian border and from the Flathead River to the Livingston Range, burning 23,000 acres. Careless campers started fires that charred 8,000 acres up both shores of Bowman Lake to the Numa and Quartz ridges. Dozens of small fires blazed over the western slopes. More than 7,600 acres burned above Nyack and 4,000 acres at Red Eagle. The Ole Creek drainage, Fielding, and the southeastern corner of the park as far as Midvale (East Glacier) were also blackened. A spot fire leaped in from the Whitefish Range across the North Fork of the Flathead River and torched 19,000 acres along Camas, Dutch, and Anaconda creeks.

Major Logan Takes Charge
Just as the Camas, Dutch, and Anaconda creek fires erupted in late August, Maj. William R. Logan, Glacier's newly commissioned superintendent of road and trail construction, arrived.

Maj. William R. Logan, first superintendent of Glacier National Park.
Courtesy Glacier National Park Archives.

The flamboyant Major Logan was the logical choice to become the park's first superintendent. He knew the country well. He had roamed the hills and valleys for years and had accompanied geologist Raphael Pumpelly through Glacier in the 1880s. Logan also knew a little about the culture of the Plains Indians; he had served as superintendent of the Indian Training School at Fort Belknap, Montana, and was supervisor of industries at large for the Bureau of Indian Affairs.

Logan immediately took charge. He sent several companies of soldiers who had just arrived from Fort William Henry Harrison and Fort Wright, Oregon, into the mountains to fight the fires. Between reviewing fire reports and bellowing orders, he set up his park headquarters in tents at Apgar and organized a patrol of six rangers.

The war against the wildfires continued through August and into the first days of September—until the rains finally came and doused the flames. All told, 120,000 acres of Glacier National Park burned that summer.

Having proven his mettle, Logan was appointed "inspector in charge" and then, the following year, the first superintendent of Glacier National Park. He immediately began building a park headquarters, setting up communication with ranger stations, improving what roads did exist, and cutting new ones. Logan rented the cabins at Apgar as temporary headquarters and began constructing an official, permanent headquarters at Fish Creek, which would finally be completed in 1913. He extended the telephone line system to the Logging Creek Ranger Station and started a line to Sperry Glacier and over Gunsight Pass to St. Mary Lake. Then he began rebuilding the two-and-one-half mile stretch of road between Belton and Apgar, which later would connect with the Going-to-the-Sun Road.

Logan would not see his work completed. He died the following year of an unknown cause while on a trip to the East.

The First Park Rangers
The first six park rangers assigned to patrol the park for poachers and encroachers were Chief Ranger Henry Vaught, Dan Doody, Bill Burns, Frank Pierce, "Dad" Randels, and the legendary Joe Cosley. The original six were shortly joined by other rangers, the most famous being Albert "Death on the Trail" Reynolds.

Notorious Joe Cosley
A trapper, sharpshooter, woodsman, and occasional outlaw, Joe Cosley was that special breed of man destined to become a Western legend.

There was no mistaking Cosley. He cut a dashing figure in his buckskin hat decorated with a rose and his fringed vaquero sash. Of French and Ojibway Indian descent, he was born in Canada and had hunted and trapped in what was now Glacier National Park for most of his life. He was already a legend among the early settlers and explorers who knew him personally or by reputation.

Cosley was fifty percent romantic and fifty percent scoundrel. Journalist Julia Nelson, in an 1953 *Canadian Cattlemen* magazine article, wrote rather politely that "Joe loved many women, not just one, as each of them thought." It was Cosley's custom to honor his sweetheart of the moment by telling her he had named a lake or mountain for her or by carving a heart around their initials on a tree.

The charming outlaw Joe Cosley—heartbreaker, trapper, ranger, and World War I sharpshooter.
Circa 1920.
Courtesy Glacier National Park Archives.

It was also Cosley's custom to carve his name or initials on trees to mark—possibly for posterity—where he camped or worked in the wilderness. Trees bearing Cosley's unmistakable hearts and initials have been found near Blind Rivers, Ontario, and in the Belly River lakes country. A tree bearing his initials and the date of 1897 has been preserved by the National Park Service.

As a park ranger, Cosley's job was to build trails, patrol for fires, shoot marauding coyotes and cougars, count deer, bighorn sheep, and mountain goats, and prevent hunters and trappers from practicing their trade inside the park. The only problem was that when no one was looking, Cosley plied *his* former trade inside the park. About four years into his park ranger career, Cosley was caught hunting and trapping and was promptly fired.

His short-lived yet lively career as a park ranger ended about the time World War I began. He joined the Canadian Army, where his sharpshooting was put to good use, and returned a highly decorated war hero.

After the war he returned to trapping game in the northern Rockies, where he consistently managed to evade U.S. and Canadian authorities and seemed to disappear like a ghost into the wilderness.

The Man Who Captured Joe Cosley

The wily Joe Cosley couldn't hide forever. In the winter of 1928 to 1929, Cosley set up camp in the Belly River country of Glacier National Park. While Cosley was off hunting, park ranger Joe Heimes discovered Cosley's camp and decided to wait him out. It was a long, cold wait.

Joe Heimes had come west from Wisconsin in 1919, taking whatever jobs he could find along the way. He worked in Yellowstone's Old Faithful Inn as a butcher's helper until 1923. That year he went to Shelby, Montana, to see the Dempsey–Gibbons fight and then moved on to Glacier National Park to look for work. He built telephone lines to Camas Creek, worked in the park sawmill at Fish Creek, then in 1924 he took a job as a fire lookout on Huckleberry Mountain.

Lookouts had to be satisfied with their own company and be in good shape. There were no telephone lines from the mountain. If the lookout spotted a fire, he had to run down the mountain to report it.

In 1926 Heimes officially joined the ranks of park rangers and worked alone at the Belly River Station. For nearly nine months in 1927 and 1928, Heimes' only contact with other people was when he took an occasional trip down the Belly River to visit his closest neighbors at the John J. West Ranch in Canada.

Now, in 1929, Heimes was waiting in the cold to capture poacher and legend Joe Cosley. Just as Heimes was about to give up hope, Cosley wandered into camp. Heimes pounced, catching Cosley by surprise. The two men struggled. Heimes, to his own amazement, managed to come out on top. Soon two other rangers showed up, and the three took the fugitive over Gable Pass to East Glacier. The next morning

Joe Heimes near the Belly River Station.
Mel Ruder, 1961.
Courtesy Patsi Morton and Glacier National Park Archives.

they boarded the train to Belton, where Cosley was charged with poaching and tried in the same afternoon.

Heimes expected Cosley to serve a few days in jail, which might have taught him a lesson. Instead Cosley was fined $100 and given a suspended jail sentence.

Later that afternoon Heimes heard that Cosley, hoping to beat park officials to his beaver cache, was already on his way back to the Belly River.

Hoping to beat Cosley to the cache, Heimes and park ranger Tom Whitcraft left early the next morning, traveling by train to East Glacier, by Model T to the Belly River Canadian ranger station, and on snowshoes to Cosley's camp. They were convinced they would easily beat Cosley to the cache. It was a two-day hike from Belton to Cosley's camp even in the summer. In winter it would take longer.

They reckoned wrong. When the rangers arrived at the camp, all they found were tracks. The fifty-nine year-old Cosley had snowshoed across the Continental Divide in less than twenty hours, picked up his furs, and disappeared into the wilds of Alberta.

Cosley never returned to Glacier National Park, at least as far as anyone knew. He continued trapping for fifteen more years and died alone in 1944 in a cabin high in the Canadian Rockies. Cosley Lake and Cosley Ridge are named for the slippery fugitive.

Albert "Death on the Trail" Reynolds

With a nickname like "Death on the Trail," park ranger Albert Reynolds had to be a true Western character. There are several theories on how this ranger earned his name.

It was said that Reynolds was one heck of a hiker. Apparently he could walk an ordinary man and some horses to death. According to the 1955 book *Timber 'n Injuns* by C. D. O'Neil, one day in 1905 Reynolds left his cabin at the foot of Lake McDonald and walked to the head of the lake. There he learned that Dr. Lyman B. Sperry, the mountain climber and explorer for whom Sperry Glacier is named, and a party from Oberlin College had left early that morning to climb a nearby mountain.

Reynolds started up the trail after them. At 4:30 that afternoon he met the climbers, who were returning without reaching their goal. They said the mountain was too far away, and they would pack for a two-

day trip starting the next morning. Reynolds said he was planning to climb the same mountain that afternoon, and he promised the climbers that when they arrived the next day "they would find their names

Albert "Death on the Trail" Reynolds.
Circa 1910.
Courtesy Glacier National Park Archives.

written on a piece of paper and left between some rocks." Sperry and the Oberlin College climbers took Reynolds' bragging with a grain of salt. They were especially certain the old man was nothing more than a blowhard when later that night he stopped by their campfire and exchanged pleasantries.

The next morning the Oberlin party started out early; they reached the top of the mountain that evening. Greeting them at the top was Reynolds' note sandwiched between two rocks. He had scribbled their names and approximate heights and weights.

There are other stories about how he got his nickname. Some say "Death on the Trail" referred to Reynolds' vow to die in his beloved backcountry.

Others cite the story of how in 1913 the sixty-five-year-old Reynolds was snowshoeing ten miles a day in the fierce snow and cold that often blankets Glacier in winter. His feet developed frostbite and, according to his journal, began "rotting." On January 30 he walked seventeen miles from his cabin south of Goat Haunt to the cabin of Kootenai Brown, a longtime friend and the acting superintendent of Canada's Waterton Lakes National Park.

Brown's diary for February 4 included the notation, "Reynolds very sick. Up all night with him." Brown realized Reynolds needed more medical attention than he could receive at Waterton and the two men started the trip to Pincher Creek, Alberta.

But Albert "Death on the Trail" Reynolds' long walk was over. The Glacier National Park ranger died on February 8, 1913.

Louis W. Hill Builds a Park

In the early years of the park, there was little that Louis Hill's Great Northern Railway did not build, finance, control, or influence.

The U.S. Congress had made Glacier a national park, but it did not provide funds for constructing facilities to accommodate visitors. The desire, the power, and the wherewithal to build the hotels, chalets, roads, and trails we still enjoy today came from Louis Warren Hill and the Great Northern Railway.

Louis Hill was the son of the legendary Empire Builder James J. Hill, who built the Great Northern Railway. He succeeded his father as president of the railroad in 1907 and found his calling as the Godfather of Glacier. He used his influence with Congress as heir to the Hill empire to help push through the bill that made Glacier a national park. When that goal was realized, he set out to bring to Glacier the comforts wealthy Easterners enjoyed in other national parks and recreational areas.

Louis Hill envisioned Glacier's alpine grandeur as America's Swiss Alps. It was an intriguing comparison—and a practical one. It had the potential to draw wealthy tourists, who traditionally vacationed in Europe, to instead take his Great Northern trains to Glacier National Park.

Between 1910 and 1913 he commissioned nine Swiss-style chalets to be built around Glacier. They were constructed at Belton, Cut Bank, Granite Park, Gunsight Lake, Many Glacier, Two Medicine, St. Mary, Sperry, and Going-to-the-Sun at Sun Point. The grand Glacier Park Hotel was built at Midvale (now East Glacier).

While his chalets and the lodge were being built, Hill contracted to set up tent camps throughout the park, most of them near the planned chalet sites. In addition he contracted for permanent tent camps at Red Eagle Lake, Goat Haunt, Cosley Lake, and Fifty Mountain.

At the time Hill was constructing the chalets, there were very few trails or roads. The new national park needed stage roads and horseback trails to transport the hoped-for tourists from chalet to chalet. The Department of the Interior had allotted very little money to Glacier National Park, so the Great Northern initially financed many of the early roads and trails.

In 1912 Hill brought in Banff outfitters William and James Brewster to set up a saddle horse and stagecoach concession to transport tourists between tent camps. He also contracted with Capt. William Swanson to build boats to ferry sightseeing tourists on the park's scenic lakes and rivers in 1916.

The Great Northern Railway designed and built

The See America First slogan came into use in 1914 and was used to draw wealthy Eastern tourists to visit the West instead of vacationing in Europe.
Courtesy California State Railroad Museum and Burlington Northern–Santa Fe Railway. 1914. CSRM # 24616T.

The Great Northern Railway's chairman of the board, Louis W. Hill, in front of the Glacier Park Hotel in 1924.
Courtesy Minnesota Historical Society and Burlington Northern–Santa Fe Railway. MHS Portrait Collection CN4.

Clarence Speed shows off the 18.5-pound trout he caught in St. Mary Lake. The photo was included in the 1913 brochure titled "Glacier National Park, Where the Fighting Trout Leap High."
Archives and Special Collections, The University of Montana–Missoula, and Burlington Northern–Santa Fe Railway.

Tepee or tent camps were set up in scenic areas around the park to house guests. While the Swiss-style chalets promoted Glacier as the Alps of America, the tepees touted the park as the home of the Blackfeet.
Archives and Special Collections, The University of Montana–Missoula, and Burlington Northern–Santa Fe Railway.

most of the early trails and wagon roads in the park to take tourists to scenic points and to connect the growing number of facilities being built. In 1912 the railroad constructed a 4.8-mile spur road from the village of St. Mary on the park's eastern border to Roes Creek inside the park. Later this spur road was realigned as part of the Going-to-the-Sun Road.

During the same year, the railroad also constructed a rough thirty-four-mile dirt road that ran through the Blackfeet Reservation. This road, which later became part of the Blackfeet Highway, connected the Great Northern Railway station at Midvale (East Glacier) to the spur road into the park and to the tourist facilities at Swiftcurrent. The National Park Service later reimbursed the railroad for the construction of the St. Mary spur and eventually rebuilt the road.

In 1914 Hill arranged with the White Motor Company to provide auto-bus services in the park, and in 1915 White formed the Glacier Park Transportation Company to operate the buses.

Overwhelmed by his own success in bringing business to Glacier, Hill decided in 1914 that he could not continue to personally manage everything in the park in the manner he had been—which was in minute, fussy detail, right down to selecting the flowers for the flower beds. He formed the Glacier Park Hotel Company, hired managers and staff, and took an oversight role for himself.

He then contracted for the construction of the Many Glacier Hotel, which opened in 1915, and the Prince of Wales Hotel in Waterton, which opened in 1927. He authorized his Glacier Hotel Company to buy John Lewis' Glacier Hotel on Lake McDonald that same year in anticipation of the completion of the Going-to-the-Sun Road. By 1930 the Great Northern Railway owned the facility and renamed it Lake McDonald Hotel.

By 1917 the Great Northern Railway had spent more than double the amount the government had to develop Glacier National Park. By the late 1920s the railroad had invested a total of more than $2.3 million.

While Hill was busy developing the park, he had his best Great Northern Railway advertising agents producing advertising. The creators of the impressive time tables, pamphlets, calendars, and railroad menu designs settled on three themes: "See America First," "Glacier's Care-killing Scenery," and "Living the Western Adventure in the Home of the Blackfeet Indians."

Louis Hill resigned as chairman of the board of the Great Northern Railway in 1929. He had done the job he set out to do. He had built hotels, chalets, camps, riding and walking trails, and roads throughout the park. Visitors could enjoy the scenic wonders and Western adventure of Glacier in rustic elegance. Louis Hill had built a park.

America's Switzerland
Louis Hill built Swiss-style hotels and chalets throughout Glacier, and visitors flocked to these retreats, which were nestled amid dramatic mountains and on the shores of pristine lakes.

Belton Chalet
The first chalet was built just outside the park and opened on June 27, 1910, barely two months after Glacier became a national park. Two cottages were added in 1911, and a large dormitory, now the lodge, was constructed in 1913. A pergola connected the chalet to the 1909 Belton Station.

Belton Chalet architectural illustration. Courtesy James Jerome Hill Collection, Minnesota Historical Society.

Belton Chalet luggage label. Courtesy Glacier National Park Archives.

Belton Chalet. Courtesy Glacier National Park Archives.

Train Fare
Round-trip fare on the Great Northern Railway from St. Paul, Minnesota: **$35.00**

Lodging
Glacier National Park Hotels and Chalets: **$3.00 per day**. With bath, **$4.00 to $5.00 per day.**

An early Great Northern Railway brochure urging tourists to visit the park. It delivered the message but was far less impressive than the stunning advertising brochures that would be produced in the following years by the Great Northern Railway. Archives and Special Collections, The University of Montana–Missoula, and Burlington Northern–Santa Fe Railway.

Glacier Park Lodge circa 1916.
Library of Congress, Prints and Photographs Division.

The construction of the Glacier Park Hotel circa 1913.
Courtesy John Chase.

Glacier Park Hotel, Now Glacier Park Lodge

Seventy-five men constructed the massive Glacier Park Hotel without the benefit of power tools, chain saws, derricks, or cranes—just simple hand tools. The massive upright logs of the hotel were cut in Washington and Oregon in the winter of 1910 and brought to Montana on flatcars. The railroad did not have equipment that could lift the logs off the flatcars, so they extended the railroad tracks and brought the logs directly to the construction site. They then used a system of pulleys to maneuver the logs into their vertical positions. The imposing Glacier Park Hotel opened on June 15, 1913.

A photographer jokingly gives three construction employees the titles of Sheriff, Horse Thief, and Outlaw—as well as hangman's nooses for the latter two. Housing known as Dirty Row was provided for workers during construction.
From the Jean Juvik Bell Collection. Courtesy John Chase.

Guests gather around the "campfire" at the Glacier Park Hotel.
Courtesy Montana Historical Society, Helena, Montana.

New Mammoth Mountain Hotel, the "Many Glacier," in the heart of Glacier National Park, on the shores of beautiful Lake McDermott, facing Grinnell Mountain, Gould Mountain, Mount Wilbur and adjacent glaciers.

Many Glacier Hotel postcard.
Ray Djuff Collection.

Many Glacier Hotel

Louis Hill chose the Swiftcurrent/Many Glacier Valley to build the largest of his hotels. The Many Glacier Hotel has 240 guest rooms in its Main and Annex wings. The Cross of Helvetia (a white cross on a scarlet shield) is Many Glacier's coat of arms, and it hangs on the door of every room. The Many Glacier Hotel opened on July 4, 1915.

Many Glacier Hotel.
Courtesy Glacier National Park Archives.

In this posed shot, Blackfeet watch as the finishing touches are put on the Many Glacier Hotel.

George Grant.
Courtesy Glacier National Park Archives (Grant 842).

Prince of Wales Hotel

Prohibition in the 1920s revived Louis Hill's earlier notion to build a hotel on the shores of Waterton Lakes National Park in Alberta. Alcohol had been legal in Alberta since 1923. Great Northern Railway officials reasoned that a resort hotel in Waterton with a legal pub would entice thirsty passengers to take their railroad to its facilities in Glacier and then on to the new Prince of Wales Hotel in Waterton. The hotel opened on July 25, 1927.

Colorful brochures drew visitors to Waterton Lakes National Park's Prince of Wales Hotel.
1928. Courtesy Glacier National Park Archives and Burlington Northern–Santa Fe Railway.

Constuction of Prince of Wales Hotel circa 1926. Courtesy of Minnesota Historical Society.

Construction workers pose atop the Prince of Wales Hotel circa 1926. Ray Djuff Collection.

The ninety-room Prince of Wales Hotel. Courtesy Glacier National Park Archives.

Guests were brought by boat to the Snyder Hotel, site of what would become Lake McDonald Lodge.
Courtesy Glacier National Park Archives.

Postcard showing the rustic elegance of the Lake McDonald Lodge.
Courtesy Tom Mulvaney.

Lake McDonald Lodge

Lake McDonald Lodge can trace its origins back to just before the turn of the twentieth century, more than a decade before the Great Northern Railway began building its Swiss-style hotels and chalets throughout the park.

In 1895 George Snyder built a two-story frame building with nine rooms where Lake McDonald Lodge now stands. In 1906 John Lewis acquired ownership of the Snyder Hotel and built eleven guest cabins. According to one legend, Lewis won the hotel from George Snyder in a poker game. Others speculated that Snyder was just tired of the business and wanted out.

In 1913 Lewis moved what was then the Lewis Hotel a short distance away and turned it into a general store. On the old hotel site, he built the new Glacier Hotel, copying the Swiss-style architecture of the Great Northern Railway buildings in the park. The Great Northern purchased Lewis' Glacier Hotel in 1930 and renamed it Lake McDonald Hotel.

Lake McDonald Lodge circa 1930.
Courtesy Minnesota Historical Society.

Guests gather on the porch of the building next to Snyder's Glacier House.
Courtesy Glacier National Park Archives.

The Lost Chalets

The Great Northern Railway constructed Swiss-style chalets at Gunsight, Many Glacier, Going-to-the-Sun at Sun Point (also known as Sun Camp), Two Medi-

Postcard featuring the Going-to-the-Sun Mountain and Chalets.
Courtesy Glacier National Park Archives and Burlington Northern–Santa Fe Railway.

St. Mary Chalets luggage label.
Courtesy Glacier National Park Archives.

cine, Cut Bank, St. Mary, Sperry, and Granite Park. The chalet at Gunsight was destroyed in an avalanche in 1916. All but three of Many Glacier's eight chalets were destroyed in the Heavens Peak Fire of 1936. One was previously flattened by an avalanche. During World War II the chalets at Going-to-the-Sun, Two Medicine (the main dining room is still in use as the camp store), Cut Bank, and St. Mary fell into disrepair and were torn down. The only two remaining chalets are the Sperry and Granite Park chalets.

Going-to-the-Sun Chalets

The Going-to-the-Sun Chalets were once perched 100 feet above St. Mary Lake on a promontory at the base of Goat Mountain. The only way to reach the chalets was by boat or on horseback.

The Going-to-the Sun Chalets were torn down in 1949.

Guests gather on a porch at the Going-to-the-Sun Chalets.
Courtesy Minnesota Historical Society.

St. Mary Chalet before it fell into disrepair and was torn down.
Courtesy of Montana Historical Society, Helena, Montana.

President Franklin D. Roosevelt delivered one of his Fireside Chats from Two Medicine Chalets in 1934.
Courtesy Glacier National Park Archives.

Sinopah Mountain rises above the Two Medicine Chalets. Mount Rockwell can be seen in the distance.
Courtesy Montana Historical Society, Helena, Montana.

The Two Medicine Chalets dining room featured stunning views of Two Medicine Lake.
Courtesy Minnesota Historical Society.

Two Medicine Chalets

The Two Medicine Chalets were constructed on the shore of Two Medicine Lake. The buildings had electric lights and used fireplaces for heat. There was cold running water in the rooms, and hot water was delivered in pitchers on request.

President Herbert Hoover and his party utilized Two Medicine as the "summer White House" in August 1930.

In 1934 Franklin Delano Roosevelt stayed for one day during his National Parks Year tour. The fireplace in the dining hall provided a setting for his speech that was broadcast nationwide.

Two Medicine Chalets postcard circa 1934. (Note: The postcard incorrectly identifies Sinopah Mountain as Mount Rockwell.)
Courtesy Glacier National Park Archives.

Above and right, Many Glacier Chalets before and after they burned in 1936.
Courtesy Glacier National Park Archives.

Many Glacier Chalets

In 1913, while the Many Glacier Hotel was still on the drawing board, the Great Northern Railway built a cluster of chalets a few hundred yards from the hotel site near the outlet of Lake McDermott (later renamed to Swiftcurrent Lake). The eight chalets were built to provide a resting place for those riding horseback through the park. Heavy rocks were placed on the roofs to hold them in place during the terrific winds that blow through the Swiftcurrent Valley.

One chalet was crushed in an avalanche a few years after it was built. The avalanche came from "South America," a snowfield named for its characteristic shape. The snowfield appears each spring on the slopes of Mount Altyn. The doomed chalet was completely flattened.

Most of the other chalets burned in the Heavens Peak Fire of 1936. Chalets "H" and "I," the only surviving chalets, can still be seen near Swiftcurrent Falls, where they house Many Glacier's maintenance personnel.

The somewhat sparse yet accommodating Sperry guest dormitory.
Courtesy Montana Historical Society, Helena, Montana.

Sperry Chalet luggage label.
Courtesy Glacier National Park Archives and Burlington–Northern Santa Fe Railway.

Sperry and Granite Park Chalets

Sperry and Granite Park chalets, Glacier's backcountry refuges, were built in 1913 and 1914. The two stone buildings of Sperry Chalet were built on Gunsight Mountain, two miles from Sperry Glacier. They overlook the deep valley of Sprague Creek. The Sperry Chalets are accessible only by trail.

Sperry Chalet was closed in 1992, partly as a result of environmental concerns. Rehabilitation began in 1996, and the chalet was back in operation in 1999.

Granite Park Chalet is reached by a four-mile trail from the Loop; it is 7.6 miles from Logan Pass.

The Granite Park Chalet was upgraded and reopened in 1997 as a primitive backcountry shelter.

Originally both chalets offered food and lodging services, but now overnight visitors to Granite Park Chalet must pack in food, water, and bedding to spend the night. The park sells and rents some items.

The Granite Park Chalets.
Courtesy Tom Mulvaney.

The initials of the Great Northern Railway appear on the Sperry Chalets.
Courtesy Minnesota Historical Society.

Trail Rides and Cowboy Guides

Evenings sitting around a campfire under a blanket of stars, listening to cowboys telling their tales, sleeping in a bed of boughs, waking to cool air and hot coffee—this was the adventure experience many visitors sought when they came to Glacier National Park. They wanted a true Wild West experience, and wranglers and cowboy guides were more than happy to deliver.

Cowboy guides in Glacier National Park.
Courtesy Montana Historical Society, Helena, Montana.

Oh, Give Me a Home Where the Buffalo Roam

Some visitors loved the idea of an authentic Western adventure, but others wanted a few city comforts thrown in.

In 1911 Louis Hill contracted to have a string of tepee or tent camps set up at various scenic spots along the trails from East Glacier to Lake McDonald. Saddle horse parties could then take long trips through the park without having to set up camp each night. These camps were popular—adding some comforts such as cots or real beds but preserving the rustic experience of camping in the wilderness.

Riding Along the Piikáni Trail

Riding the trails in the mountains had become a popular pastime for tourists well before Glacier became a park. Many of the trails in these mountains were once traveled by the Piikáni and other tribes that ventured across the Continental Divide to trade or hunt.

That nostalgic fact appealed to tourists who wanted to experience the Old West while viewing the magnificence of the mountains, lakes, and valleys. Riding the trails was also the only way, other than on foot, to really see Glacier.

Early organized trail rides or saddle horse concessions were operated by independent ranchers from their nearby ranches or from base camps set up inside the park.

In 1912 Louis Hill brought in Banff outfitters William and James Brewster to set up a trail ride and stagecoach concession to operate between the camps and the newly built chalets and hotels.

Brewster's stagecoach operation was terminated at the end of the season in 1914 when motorized buses came to Glacier. The following spring a number of the small, independent saddle horse outfits combined as the Park Saddle Horse Company under the leadership

Wranglers and "dudes" enjoy a meal around the campfire. Piegan Glacier in background.
Courtesy K. Ross Toole Archives and Burlington Northern–Santa Fe Railway.

Jim Whilt, Glacier trail guide and Poet of the Rockies.
Courtesy Glacier National Park Archives.

of W. N. Noffsinger, an attorney from Kalispell, Montana. The base ranch was on the Blackfeet Reservation east of the park, near Babb, Montana. The company eventually obtained a contract with the National Park Service and became the official saddle horse operator in Glacier.

The Park Saddle Horse Company continued to expand its operations under the brand "—X6" (Bar X Six). The company became the largest saddle horse outfit of its kind in the world, owning more than 1,000 head of horses and taking more than 10,000 visitors a year on the park's trails.

They Called Themselves "Dude Wranglers"

I am going to set down a few facts about wrangling dudes, before my candle sputters out into utter darkness. First of all, a guide must dress Western—big hat, chaps, spurs, tough rag and what have you—be mannerly, courteous and, in fact, he should show a glint of human intelligence even though he is not housebroke.
—Jim Whilt in Giggles from Glacier Guides, 1935

Some were big and husky, and some were small and wiry. Some drank too much, and some didn't

drink at all. What they shared was a knowledge of horses and the backcountry—and a healthy sense of humor.

One of Glacier's best-known wranglers was Jim Whilt, who moonlighted as a poet and authored *Giggles from Glacier Guides*, a collection of stories from cowboy guides. Jim tells his own story best:

Having been an utter failure in all other lines of work and having never attended school but three days—two days the teacher wasn't there and the other day I wasn't—my education did not work on myself as I have noticed in so many cases, going to their heads and leaving their hands useless. So here in Glacier Park, God's own outdoors, God's and mine, myself and sixty others take the dudes over the trails and tell them some of the facts about this land of shining mountains for a period of three months. Then our work begins. We have to go over the entire park, shut off the waterfalls, fold up the switch-backs, brand all the young sheep and goats, dig all the dens for the bears, teach the little fish to swim and plant them in different lakes and streams. The latter is a hard job, for in the fall the water is hard and digging the holes is an arduous task.

After his wrangling days were done, Jim Whilt became well known as the Poet of the Rockies.

Edwina Noffsinger, who helped her husband George run the Park Saddle Horse Company after his father W. N. Noffsinger died in 1924, said in an 1982 interview with Mary Murphy that

George did have cowboys that worked...endeared themselves to people, and year after year they would ask for them. Well, Ace Powell was a cowboy, and extremely unreliable. He would get his dudes up in the park, and they'd get a-drinking, or he'd lose his horses. They turned them loose in those days, hobbled or with a bell mare. They would go out at four o'clock in the morning and round them up and bring them in. Ace would lose his horses. Year after year, George would say he wouldn't have Ace back again. But he always did.

Ace Powell may have "lost his horses" while sketching scenes or drawing animals. He would go on to

"Where men are men . . . You'll find true Westerners out here. They take things as they come—and you'll soon fall into the same live-one-day-at-a-time state of mind." This image and quote appeared in a 1935 Great Northern Railway brochure advertising trail riding.
Courtesy K. Ross Toole Archives and Burlington Northern–Santa Fe Railway.

Glacier trail guide and nationally known Western artist Asa L. "Ace" Powell, who lived most of his life in Glacier National Park.
Ace Powell. Courtesy Glacier National Park Archives.

Trail riders near Swiftcurrent Pass. This photograph appeared in a 1935 Great Northern Railway brochure advertising trail riding.
Courtesy K. Ross Toole Archives and Burlington Northern–Santa Fe Railway.

Trail riders in Glacier National Park.
Courtesy Glacier National Park Archives.

Two black bear cubs named Pete and Repeat were among the most popular of Ace Powell's Glacier National Park drawings.
Ace Powell.
Courtesy Glacier Natural History Association.

become a nationally known western artist.

According to Edwina Noffsinger, Blacky Dillon was another wrangler that George Noffsinger would fire every year and then hire in the spring because "some dude had written and wanted him. All of these unreliable people were charming, you know."

Blacky Dillon was a wrangler at Many Glacier. He had a thick black beard and was said to almost always smell of horse manure and alcohol. He also had a terrific flair for the theatrical. Blacky would burst through the doors of the Many Glacier Hotel wearing a long, black operatic cape that he would sweep about him as he paraded toward the bar. A tourist once asked, "Blacky, where did your get your costume?" Indignant, Blacky answered in his best Shakespearean voice, "Lady, this is no costume! These are my clothes!"

Blacky also had a hand in Many Glacier's only recorded riot. He and two cowboys were drinking late one evening in the downstairs bar. The cowboys were getting rowdy, and the security guard asked that they finish their beers by midnight and leave. Blacky was ready to do just that, but the cowboys ignored the guard. The infuriated guard whisked the bottles away and was promptly attacked by the cowboys. Five airmen who were seated nearby and several hotel employees leaped into the fight—on the guard's side of the ruckus. Blacky considered himself a peaceable fel-

low and crawled under a table. During a lull in the fight, the cowboys escaped. They were captured later when they returned to beat up Blacky for not coming to their assistance.

Blacky was hired and fired every year for decades. When he was too old to wrangle, he drove a four-horse "tally-ho" the three miles between the Many Glacier Hotel and the Swiftcurrent Auto Camp. One day, a slightly inebriated and somewhat bored Blacky cracked his whip on the horses' rumps, sending them into a wild gallop. The several elderly ladies who were tossed about the coach screamed in terror until Blacky finally pulled the runaway horses to a stop. During the fiasco the tally-ho struck and damaged the wrangler boss's new car. He didn't take it very well, and poor Blacky was fired for the last time.

Blacky Dillon left Glacier and lived out his remaining years performing as a stagecoach robber at Knott's Berry Farm in California.

Cruising Glacier

During Glacier National Park's first decade, it became clear that boats were more convenient than stages or wagons for transporting tourists and supplies to the hotels and other scenic spots.

The Whitney *and the* Emeline

In 1895 George Snyder, who built the Snyder House hotel at the head of Lake McDonald, purchased a

The Emeline.
Courtesy Glacier National Park Archives.

forty-foot steamboat in Wisconsin and had it loaded on a Great Northern train and hauled to Belton. Meanwhile, Snyder and the Apgars widened and corduroyed (laid logs side by side to create a road surface) the stage road from the Middle Fork of the Flathead River to Lake McDonald to portage the boat to the lake.

He christened it the *F. I. Whitney* in honor of the Great Northern agent whose clever pamphlets, train schedules, and booklets invited tourists to take the Great Northern Railway to see Lake McDonald.

The *F. I. Whitney* was the first known commercial craft to cruise any of Glacier's lakes. It ferried passengers and supplies back and forth from Apgar at the foot of Lake McDonald to the Snyder Hotel at the head of the lake.

In 1906 Frank Kelly, who lived in a cabin on the lake, built the thirty-five-foot *Emeline* to take guests on tours around the lake. The two-boat Lake McDonald fleet grew to five by 1910.

In 1914 John Lewis, who had acquired the Snyder Hotel in 1906 and renamed it the Glacier Hotel, offered to purchase the sixty-foot *City of Polson* from Bill Swanson, a boat builder and operator on Flathead Lake. Swanson's business on Flathead Lake was in decline and he agreed to the sale. The deal required delivery of the boat to Lake McDonald, which proved to be no easy task.

The Rising Wolf *at Two Medicine Lake.*
George Grant, 1932.
Courtesy Glacier National Park Archives.

The Lewtana.
Courtesy Glacier National Park Archives.

Courtesy John Chase and Burlington Northern–Santa Fe Railway.

Moving the City of Polson

Swanson recounted his experiences navigating the Flathead River from Flathead Lake to Lake McDonald in a June 1970 story written by Phyllis Clark in the *Daily Inter-Lake* newspaper in Kalispell, Montana: "We headed up river June 15 during high water. I had a green crew of six men—each hired for a dollar a day and board. It took about two weeks."

At first the trip was largely uneventful—until the boat ran aground on a gravel bar in the middle of the river near Bad Rock Canyon. As the crew backed off the bar, the boat hit rocks, knocking a propeller loose. The next morning the crew fished the propeller out of the river and reattached it, but the boat was stuck in rock and gravel and wouldn't budge.

Swanson sent the engineer upriver in a "tender" (a small rowboat) to tie one end of a line to a large tree and let out the line as he returned to the grounded *City of Polson*. On the way back the tender floated in too fast, bounced off the bow of the *Polson*, and sank. The crewmen managed to catch the thrashing engineer with a pike pole and pull him aboard, but they couldn't save the tender.

Losing the tender was a problem. There was no way to get to shore without it, except to swim. Swanson and the crew built a makeshift boat out of wood scavenged onboard the *Polson* and floated it to shore. From there, Swanson walked to the small town of Columbia Falls and bought lumber and material for a new tender, which they built the next day.

"The trip up the river took us through Red Lick Rapids, and some folks said we'd never make it—can't get through," Swanson recalled. "We had 1,800 feet of steel cable, and I fastened it to a rock and ran the cable along the riverbank. We picked up the end and used a winch to wind the boat over the swift current. It took about fifteen minutes to get through, then we went fishing."

Before they finally reached Apgar, they had to pull through fifteen more gravel bars, gouging deep channels as they passed.

When the boat was launched on Lake McDonald, it was christened the *Lewtana,* for John Lewis.

The DeSmet on Lake McDonald.
Courtesy Tom Mulvaney.

Swanson captained the *Lewtana* until Louis Hill's Glacier Park Hotel Company contracted with him to build and operate tour boats for the park. He built many of the boats that cruised Glacier's lakes, including the forty-passenger *Rising Wolf,* later renamed *Sinopah,* which cruised Two Medicine Lake, the *DeSmet* on Lake McDonald, the sixty-three-foot *International* on Waterton Lake, the *St. Mary* on St. Mary Lake, and the *Little Chief,* which was added to the Two Medicine fleet.

Consolidating the Fleets

For several years there were at least three separate boat concessions in Glacier, and ownership rotated through the years. The boat operations on Lake McDonald that began in 1895 with George Snyder's *F. I. Whitney* were eventually transferred to the Glacier Park Transportation Company. In 1911 both James T.

A passenger boat brings guests to the Going-to-the-Sun Chalets.
Courtesy Tom Mulvaney.

The St. Mary *cruises the lake of the same name.*
Courtesy Glacier National Park Archives.

Maher and the Glacier Park Hotel Company had boats floating on St. Mary Lake to take guests, staff, and supplies to Sun Point. Ten years later Bill Swanson's boat concession for the Glacier Park Hotel Company had launches cruising Two Medicine and Swiftcurrent lakes and in 1927 their flagship—the *International* was floating on Waterton Lake.

In 1938 Swanson sold it to Arthur J. Burch and Carl Anderson of Kalispell, who operated the enterprise as the Glacier Park Boat Company. By 1985 the company had consolidated all the boat operations in Glacier and had nine boats sailing on six lakes. The *International* and the Waterton Lakes operation were later sold to Shoeline Cruise Company of Alberta.

Gear Jammers and the First Tour Buses

The predecessor's of today's red tour buses, or "reds," Glacier's early buses began replacing stagecoaches in 1915. These buses, affectionately called "jammers" or "jammer buses"—and their drivers, known as "gear jammers"—are a beloved part of Glacier National Park history.

The First Buses

In 1913 Walter White of the White Motor Company convinced Louis Hill that motorized buses could

The boat Chief Two Guns *on Lake Josephine.*
Courtesy Montana Historical Society, Helena, Montana.

One of the original Glacier buses awaits passengers at the Glacier Park Hotel.
T. J. Hileman, circa 1915.
Courtesy Montana Historical Society, Helena, Montana.

Buses cross the old St. Mary Bridge.
T. J. Hileman, circa 1915. Courtesy Glacier National Park Archives.

transport visitors around Glacier at least as well and probably better than the stagecoaches then being used. Hill agreed to test White's vehicles for the 1914 season, and in mid-June ten eleven-passenger buses, five touring cars, and a couple of two-ton trucks arrived by railroad at the Glacier Park Station at Midvale (East Glacier). There were no garage storage or repair facilities; the operators would just have to "make do" for the season.

The 1914 buses were black, open-top buses with canvas tops that could be pulled forward in case of rain. The tops hooked to the windshield with long straps that extended down to the front fenders to hold the canvas in place. Instead of a door on the driver's side, there was a spare tire and a tank, so the driver had to climb over the tire and tank to get into the bus. The headlights were illuminated by acetylene gas. When the skies grew dark, the gear jammer had to stop the bus, get out, and turn the knob on the gas tank on the left fender, which fed the acetylene line to the headlights. Then they lit the headlights with a match.

Heavily loaded with carefree sightseeing passengers traveling over rough, rocky stagecoach roads,

A Glacier bus climbs the Going-to-the-Sun Road.
Courtesy of Minnesota Historical Society.

these early buses had their fair share of problems: flat tires, failed differentials, overheating engines, and other auto breakdowns. In the spring and early fall,

A gear jammer poses in front of two early-day Glacier National Park buses.
Courtesy John Chase.

the buses frequently became mired in mud and had to be pulled out by teams of horses.

Goodbye Stagecoaches, Hello Buses

Americans have had a love affair with automobiles since the first Duryea chugged forth from a bicycle shop in Massachusetts. So it was no surprise that tourists who embraced America's new motorized transportation outnumbered the nostalgic few who still enjoyed the rough and tumble ride of the stagecoaches and the feel of the Old West. The general consensus of the Glacier Park Hotel Company was that buses were more desirable and practical for taking sightseers through the park than stagecoaches.

With the top down, passengers enjoy the view from an early bus.
Courtesy Glacier National Park Archives.

Toward the end of the trial season for the first buses, Hill released the Brewster brothers from their contract to provide stagecoach services in the park.

The following year Hill signed an agreement with Walter White to provide transportation services in Glacier using White Motor Company equipment. White and his business partner Roe Emery organized the Glacier Park Transportation Company, and in 1915 White's buses became the park's public transportation.

A Blackfeet named Lazy Boy at the wheel of an early Glacier Park Transportation Company tour bus.
Courtesy Montana Historical Society, Helena, Montana.

Gear Jammers

"Whenever we had to change grades when going up the mountain road or coming down, we had to shift from one gear to another, and we had to do that by double clutching," said Robert L. Wise, a 1936 gear jammer. "If you did it correctly there was just harmony, it was just silent . . . but if you fouled up there was a loud noise of the gears. That's why we were called gear jammers."

Most of the gear jammers were young college men working in the park during the summer. Each wore a uniform of gray whipped-cord britches, a gray shirt and blue tie, polished English cavalry boots, a blue pea coat, and a cap. They were a dashing lot lined up in front of their buses.

Beneath Going-to-the-Sun Mountain, a gas shovel and trucks remove rock from the excavation site for the Going-to-the-Sun Road.
Courtesy Glacier National Park Archives

7

Roaring through the Twenties
1920–1929

T HE 1920S GAVE AMERICANS BABE RUTH, *jazz, airmail service, fledgling airlines, cars, radios, and movies with sound. Women secured the right to the vote, prohibition became the law of the land, and speakeasies were the place to be. Record numbers of visitors came to Glacier in the 1920s, a decade marked by continued efforts to draw tourists and make their travel more enjoyable. The Old West and the Blackfeet Indians became symbols of the Great Northern Railway's campaign to lure tourists to the park.*

Hundreds of young men and women flocked to Glacier to work in the hotels and restaurants nestled in the wilderness, ranger-led nature walks and campfire talks became popular, and an incredible feat of engineering was achieved in the construction of the mighty Going-to-the-Sun Road.

The Old West is Still in the
Saddle at Glacier National Park

Americans' romantic view of the Old West was as strong as ever, and it became the theme of the Great Northern Railway's campaign to lure tourists to Glacier. Brilliantly designed brochures were distributed in the United States and around the world declaring that the Old West was still alive in Glacier National Park—the home of the Blackfeet Indians.

Louis Hill commissioned artists Kathryn Leighton, Julius Seyler, and W. Langdon Kihn to paint portraits

of the Blackfeet. But the artist most identified with the Blackfeet of Glacier National Park was Winold Reiss.

The German-born Reiss studied art at the Munich Academy. He immigrated to the U.S. in 1913 with his own romantic image of the American West. His goal was to study the American Indian; he chose the Blackfeet tribe. In 1919 Reiss came to Glacier National Park for a three-week visit. During that time he completed thirty-five portraits of the Blackfeet. His dignified portraits earned the respect of the Blackfeet, and they honored him with a ceremony, bestowing on him the Indian name of Ksistakpoka—Beaver Child.

In 1927 Louis Hill commissioned Reiss to paint portraits of the Blackfeet for the Great Northern Railway. Reiss completed fifty-one portraits that year and returned to Glacier several more times to paint more portraits.

The Winold Reiss paintings were used on Great

Great Northern Railway magazine ads from the 1920s.
Courtesy John Chase and Burlington Northern–Santa Fe Railway.

Winold Reiss paints Medicine Boss Ribs, a Blackfeet tribe member, in 1931.
T. J. Hileman, circa 1931. Archives and Special Collections, The University of Montana–Missoula, and Burlington Northern–Santa Fe Railway.

Winold Reiss portraits of Many Guns (top) and Black Boy and Ragged Woman (bottom).
(Top) Winold Reiss, Many Guns, mixed media on Whatman board, 39 x 26", 1948 collection of Burlington Northern–Santa Fe Railway. (Bottom) Winold, The Pemmican Makers (Cecile Black Boy and Ragged Woman), mixed media on Whatman board, 52 x 30", 1934 Anschutz Collection.

Northern Railway calendars for over thirty years. They were also used on dining car and hotel menus, ink blotters, playing cards, postcards, and brochures about Glacier National Park.

Winold Reiss died in 1953 following a series of strokes. In July 1954 the Blackfeet held a ceremony at Red Blanket Butte near Chief Mountain to honor him. George Bullchild led the group of mourners in traditional prayers and songs, then friends and family scattered Reiss' ashes to the wind.

Highway to the Sky

In 1924 four horsemen rode over the Continental Divide. Stopping a few miles west of Logan Pass, they dismounted and stood on the mountaintop to take in the view. Above them stood the vertical peaks of the Garden Wall; below, the green valley of Logan Creek wound through the mountains toward Belton. This seemingly ordinary event was in fact a critical moment for the future of Glacier National Park.

Americans loved their automobiles, and the public was clamoring for new roads to be built to every corner of the nation. Since the day Stephen Mather had been appointed the director of the National Park Service in 1916, he had been fighting for better roads in the national parks. By 1924 he started to see some real results: the U.S. Congress had passed legislation authorizing a whopping $7.5 million for roads, trails, and bridges in national parks over the following three years. Now Mather was faced with the crucial decision of where to build a road through the heart of Glacier National Park.

Mather feared that a poorly planned road would

Engineers near the present-day Loop look over the terrain along Haystack Butte toward Logan Pass.
Courtesy Glacier National Park Archives.

Looking southeast.

Cliffs west of Oberlin.

Future site of Triple Arches.

In Frank A. Kittredge's 1925 Survey Report, the line (changed to red for clarity) drawn across the October 1924 photographs (these pages) indicates the future route of the Going-to-the-Sun Road.
Courtesy Glacier National Park Archives.

Granite cliffs east of Logan Pass.

damage the land it was built to showcase. He vowed that wouldn't happen: "Our purpose is to construct only such roads as contribute solely toward accessibility of the major scenic areas by motor without disturbing the solitude and quiet of other sections."

The route of Glacier's famous Going-to-the-Sun Road was decided on that mountaintop in 1924 when Thomas Vint, a wet-behind-the-ears National Park Service (NPS) landscape architect, stepped forward to oppose veteran road-building engineer George E. Goodwin's plan to build a road that rose to the summit of Logan Pass in a series of fifteen switchbacks. Vint said that Goodwin's fifteen switchbacks would make the landscape "look like miners had been in there." Then he turned to Stephen Mather and Charles Kraebel, the new superintendent of Glacier National Park, and proposed a longer road that rose along the face of the Garden Wall in a single switchback. "If this roadway could be benched into the sedimentary rock of the Garden Wall all the way down the valley,"

he noted, "the scene below would be preserved completely untouched."

After seeking other opinions, Mather concluded that Vint's proposed road would more effectively preserve the scenic landscape.

Building the road into the rock face of the Garden Wall would be a monumental engineering project. It required the brightest landscape architects and en-

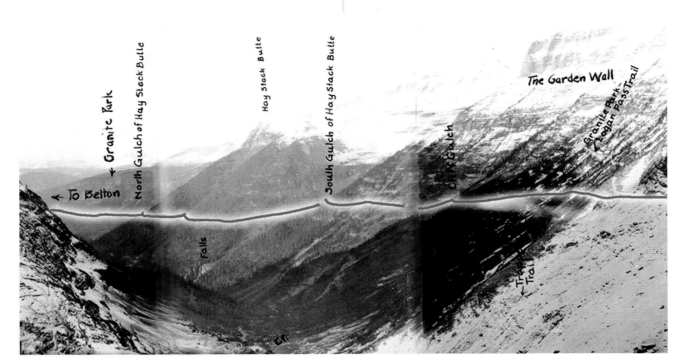

Looking west from near Oberlin Bend.

Future site of the east-side tunnel.

gineers in the NPS. The project also needed the expertise of Bureau of Public Roads (BPR) engineers to ensure the road met the bureau's standards for road construction. An agreement between the NPS and the BPR was formed that established collaboration of these two agencies during planning and construction. This agreement set a policy for all future National Park Service roads and is still in effect today.

The road on the west side of the Continental Divide had to be benched into the sheer sides of the Garden Wall, which was a daunting task in itself. What made it infinitely more difficult to build than other roads across the rugged Rocky Mountains was the National Park Service's edict to "protect the landscape" above all else. Most of the work had to be done with hand tools to reduce the impact on the land.

Construction of the 12.5-mile West Side Road from Logan Creek to the summit of Logan Pass began in June 1925. Led by Archie R. Douglas, the on-site boss for the Williams and Douglas Construction Company, the first sixty rough-hewn men came to Logan Creek and hastily built a headquarters camp. While walls were being nailed together at the Logan Creek camp site, trail crews were already hiking up the mountains to clear access trails for road construction crews and pack strings of horses, which were hauling lumber, drilling steel, explosives, tools, compressors, and food.

At the peak of construction, 300 men were scattered along the mountainsides engaged in brutally hard and dangerous work. Field engineers dangled from ropes 1,000 feet down a mountainside to triangulate and stake the alignment of the future road. "Powder monkeys" (explosive experts) were lowered over the face of the Garden Wall on ropes tied to trees to drill holes and set dynamite. Tunnel crews drilled, blasted, and jack-hammered the 192-foot-long, 18-foot-high West Side Tunnel through the mountain above McDonald Creek. Talented mountain engineers and skilled construction crews forged a jagged mountain outcropping into the graceful 75-foot-radius Loop that turned the Going-to-the-Sun Road from its northwesterly direction eastward to climb along the Garden Wall. Stonemasons built impressive bridges and retaining walls, such as the Triple Arches.

There were numerous injuries, but only one man was killed during the construction of the West Side Road. Charles Rudberg, the trail crew foreman, was killed in June 1926 when he lost his grip while descending the cliffs about a mile above The Loop and fell sixty feet.

The men who built the Going-to-the-Sun Road were an interesting hodgepodge of Americans and Swedes, Austrians and Russians. Some were seasoned road builders, while others were World War I veterans, young men from nearby farms, or European immigrants eager for experience and a new start in life. Some were hired for their special skills, such as the sixteen Russian stonemasons who built the rock retaining walls, including the Triple Arches. Despite an occasional squabble and differences in skills, language, and dispositions, the men got along well. They took a robust pleasure in the hard work and the risks, recounting them in glorious detail in the evening over coffee, tea, or whiskey.

These hearty men completed the West Side Road on October 20, 1928. The following spring the road

Hauling supplies on the Mount Cannon section of the road in 1926.
Construction report by W. G. Peters.
Courtesy Glacier National Park Archives.

In this 1924 Going-to-the-Sun Road construction camp photograph, meat is strung high across a pole, well out of the bears' reach, with a determined "cookie" standing guard.
Courtesy Glacier National Park Archives.

An October 1928 view of the construction of the Triple Arches.
Courtesy Glacier National Park Archives.

These men are using "go-devils," or horse-drawn travois, to haul culvert pipes, steel rails, and air pipes on the old Granite Park Trail in 1926.
Construction Report by W.G. Peters.
Courtesy Glacier National Park Archives.

Stone rubble retaining walls and guard walls along cliff section near The Loop in 1927.
Construction Report by W.G. Peters. Courtesy Glacier National Park Archives.

View of construction on east portal of the west-side tunnel.
Construction Report by W.G. Peters. Courtesy Glacier National Park Archives.

699 Interior of Tunnel — Logan Pass Highway

The cave-like interior of the west-side tunnel, completed in 1927.
R.E. Marble, Photographer. Courtesy Glacier National Park Archives.

to Logan Pass was opened to an appreciative public on June 15, 1929. Nearly 14,000 automobiles traveled the road from West Glacier to Logan Pass that year.

The Ranger Naturalists

Naturalists began taking on an important role in the park in 1921 when M. P. Somes, a concessionaire, started conducting walking tours to explain the geology, flora, and fauna of Glacier for a fee. The following year Dr. Morton J. Elrod, a seasonal park employee of the University of Montana, started a free nature guide service—providing a series of nature walks and self-guided nature trails. He published *Elrod's Guide,* the first guidebook for the park, which sold for many years as the official park guide. After 1926 Elrod's guide service was called the Ranger Naturalist Service.

In 1929 Dr. George C. Ruhle was appointed the park's first permanently assigned NPS naturalist and was put in charge of the Ranger Naturalists. He laid out nature trails and created campfire programs at the campgrounds.

George C. Ruhle

George Ruhle was on a path to becoming a noted scientist. He had a doctorate in nuclear physics and at

Cover of a 1935 Ranger Naturalist Service brochure.
Courtesy Glacier National Park Archives.

George Ruhle on horseback near Stoney Indian Pass.
George Grant, 1932. Courtesy Glacier National Park Archives.

George C. Ruhle dedicating the library named in his honor in 1974.
NPS, 1975. Courtesy Glacier National Park Archives.

age twenty-six was head of the University of Oklahoma's physics and chemistry department. But in 1926, when he started working for the National Park Service to bolster his income, he discovered his true calling as a naturalist.

"I started out as a 'posie picker' in Yosemite. Then they called us pansie petters and nature fakers or nature guides. The term 'naturalist' came ten years later," he said. After working in Yosemite National Park for two years, he became a ranger in Yellowstone National Park. When the National Park Service asked him to continue his service, he replied that he would if he could go to Glacier: "It was the kind of park that I wanted. I've always felt that."

Ruhle was the park naturalist at Glacier from 1929 until 1940. During that time he initiated programs aimed to challenge visitors to love and protect the park as he did. He wrote pamphlets titled "Glacial Drift" or "Nature Notes." They were simple and designed to "inculcate an interest in nature and natural things."

Ruhle established Indian names or their English translations for more than 100 mountains and lakes in Glacier. He suggested the name Going-to-the-Sun for Glacier's famous road. He wrote several books on Glacier, including his *The Ruhle Handbook, Roads and*

Trails of Waterton-Glacier National Parks, which is still used by visitors today. He established Glacier's first museum in a tent, and in 1974 Glacier's library was named the George C. Ruhle Library.

In 1961 Ruhle set up the Division of International Cooperation for the National Park Service and was known internationally as the U.S. National Park Service Ambassador. He returned often to Glacier, speaking to conservation groups and sharing his love for the park until his death in 1994.

Gladys Johnson and her friend Lenore worked as waitresses at the Glacier Park Hotel. Johnson's diary entries and personal photographs shed light on what life was like working in the park. John Chase creates Glacier National Park history displays at the Glacier Park Hotel every year featuring Johnson's adventures.
1926.
Courtesy Gladys Johnson Hasse Family and John Chase.

Beloved Vagabonds of Glacier

The roaring twenties gave rise to a new sense of freedom and the nation's first youth culture. Those under age twenty-five had a devil-may-care exuberance and a new set of attitudes that shook the senses of their more reserved parents.

The shining mountains of Glacier had always lured those with an adventurous spirit. Among the dining room staff at the Glacier Park Hotel were two such adventurers.

In the mid-1920s Gladys Johnson and her best

friend Lenore were students at Carlton College in Northfield, Minnesota. The pair worked as waitresses at the Glacier Park Hotel during the summers of 1926 and 1927.

Gladys had kept a diary since she was fourteen, and she continued to do so until she was seventy. When the summer of 1926 was over and it was time for Gladys and Lenore to head home she wrote:

> *Diary, I haven't told you of our great inspiration—have I? Lenore and I are going to be vagabonds and bum our way home and "Study Philosophy on the highway of the University of the Universe." We got our inspiration from reading* The Beloved Vagabond *by Locke.*

Gladys Johnson after a trail ride.
1926. Courtesy Gladys Johnson Hasse Family and John Chase.

Pack rats (bellhops) at the Glacier Park Hotel, 1920s. Left to right are Harold Bender, Lou Shepard, and Ralph Chase.
Circa 1925.
Courtesy Chase Family and John Chase Collection.

Glacier Speak

Glacier National Park employees developed their own slang for the jobs performed in the 1920s and 1930s.

guide	dude wrangler
bus driver	gear jammer
bellhop	pack rat
cook	dough smoker
waitress	garbage heaver
chambermaid	sheet snatcher
laundress	bubble queen

We are going home by way of Yellowstone and we aren't going to take anything with us except our toothbrushes, combs and canes. We wanted a dog, but as no dog is available we have bought ourselves canes. We think it will be the grandest lark imaginable.

We had a terrible time evading people's direct questions of how we were going home, why not [leave at] night on the Oriental Limited instead of in the morning—oh, lots of others. We were almost a couple of wrecks Sunday. The secrecy of selling our [train] tickets and of hiding the fact that we were going to bum our way home was wearing. You see, Bob had to check our trunks for us [on the train] and do that secretly too. We sold one ticket for $15.00 and divided the money.

We set out in the early morn-

ing, it was raining. We were supremely happy— thinking now of the experiences and adventures ahead and now of the astonishment and gasps of the people behind.

While walking the muddy road to Browning, a traveling salesman offered them a ride. "He already picked up two bums," Gladys wrote, "so with five in the car it was crowded." When they got to Browning, the men invited the women to hop the next freight with them. Gladys and Lenore politely declined. They spent the night with friends. The next day they went to the train station but were unable to convince the engineer to give them a free ride. So they scraped together enough money for tickets to Great Falls, Montana.

From Great Falls they hitchhiked the rest of the way home. At Gardiner, Montana, they got a ride with a husky truck driver who smoked perfumed cigarettes, and just outside Cody, Wyoming, they hitched a ride with a jovial "German Sheep King" who was returning from his morning visit to his flock. They spent some time in Yellowstone National Park looking at geysers and bears, then finally arrived home in Minnesota.

Gladys married Merten Hasse, a teacher in Aberdeen, South Dakota, and became a homemaker. She used her artistic talent to write poetry and construct marionettes, with which she entertained thousands of schoolchildren over the years.

Rum Runners and Such

Alcohol had long been a part of Glacier's history. Trappers drank it, settlers doctored with it, and traders made a handsome profit selling it to the Indians in the 1800s. In the 1900s the elegance of spirits and fine dining came to Glacier along with the hotels and chalets.

When the U.S. Congress passed the Prohibition Act in 1920—to promote sobriety, morality, and good health—it uncorked a fourteen-year spree of illegal drinking, speakeasies, and bootleggers.

When Prohibition became the law of the land,

alcohol disappeared from Glacier, or so it seemed. A covert system evolved to provide hooch to the thirsty. "Rum runners" brought alcohol from Canada—just as they had during the heyday of the whiskey forts. Everyone in "the system" got a little payoff. When a guest at one of the Glacier hotels wanted a nip, he made a discreet inquiry, and his liquid refreshment, wrapped in plain brown paper, was delivered to his door.

No official records exist to suggest that the Glacier Park Hotel Company condoned the practice or even knew it existed.

Prohibition prompted Louis Hill to build the Prince of Wales Hotel on Waterton Lake in Canada in 1927. The law did not apply there, and thirsty guests could gather around the hotel pub, have a drink, and sing songs through the night.

Prohibition was repealed in 1933, and alcohol was legally available to Glacier's guests once again.

The Bell Ringers

The Swiss custom of placing bells on mountaintops inspired advertising agents of the Great Northern Railway and the manager of the Glacier Park Hotel Company to place bells on the mountains and passes of Glacier.

The park superintendent agreed, and in 1926 beautifully toned locomotive bells were placed on the summits of Swiftcurrent and Piegan passes and on the trail above Siyeh Pass. In 1929 a fourth bell was placed on Mount Henry, where the Two Medicine Trail crosses Scenic Point.

For the next seventeen years, visitors enjoyed ringing the bells to herald their arrival to the summits. In 1943 the four bells were removed and donated to a World War II scrap metal drive.

Ralph Chase pours a nip for the Glacier Park Hotel butcher. Ralph worked as a baggage porter at the hotel and participated in "the system," which brought alcohol from Canada to the park.
Courtesy Chase Family and John Chase Collection.

Ginny Leigh rings the bell on Swiftcurrent Pass. This photograph was taken by another adventurous spirit, Rum Cashman, who worked at the Many Glacier Hotel in 1935 and 1936.
Rum Cashman, 1935.
Courtesy Rum Cashman Family and Glacier National Park Archives.

Park visitors take in the incredible views from Glacier "reds" on the Going-to-the-Sun Road circa 1935.
Courtesy Glacier National Park Archives.

8

The Tumultuous Thirties
1930 – 1939

I N THE 1930S THE GREAT DEPRESSION *held the nation in its grip. One-fourth of all American workers were unemployed, and a quarter of the nation's farmers had lost their land. Thousands of hungry men and women lined up every day to get a loaf of bread or a bowl of soup. The worst drought in U.S. history turned the Great Plains into a dust bowl, and destitute farm families trekked to California in search of work. President Franklin Delano Roosevelt's New Deal offered hope, and people across the nation struggled, endured, and prevailed.*

The only celebration of the decade was when the Prohibition Act was repealed in 1933. As the decade came to a close, Americans turned to face the gang of dictators that had taken power in Europe and threatened the world.

During these troubled times, Glacier National Park remained an island of hope—a magnificent park bustling with activity and jobs for needy people.

Glacier, however, did not totally escape the dark clouds of the 1930s. Visits to the park were at their lowest levels. The Cut Bank and St. Mary chalets and the Prince of Wales Hotel closed in 1933. The Heavens Peak Fire wiped out many of the buildings at Swiftcurrent and threatened the Many Glacier Hotel, which added to the gloom.

The Civilian Conservation Corps
In 1933, just 100 days after his inauguration, Presi-

dent Franklin D. Roosevelt launched his New Deal program to pull America out of the Great Depression. Another of his many programs was the Civilian Conservation Corps (CCC), designed to put people back to work.

The Corps was open to needy veterans of World War I and unemployed men ages eighteen to twenty-five. Each man received $30 a month, $22 of which was sent to his folks back home.

The young men of the Civilian Conservation Corps were known as "Cs," "Soil Soldiers," and "Roosevelt's Tree Army," but they didn't care. They had a bed, food, a job, and a little money, all of which were hard to get during the Depression years—especially for those without skills or trades.

Each CCC member wore a spruce-green uniform and a cap or hat emblazoned with the corps logo. They lived in barracks and worked under near-military

discipline on controlling floods and erosion, building roads and fire lookouts, planting trees, combating forest-destroying insects, and maintaining trails and campsites in parks throughout the nation.

In the first month of the corps, eight CCC tent camps were set up in Glacier, and between 50 and 250 men were assigned to each camp. Before long there were fourteen main camps and numerous "spike" camps of small crews.

Crews immediately went to work building barracks to replace some of the tent camps. Many of these young Soil Soldiers were sent out to fell dead trees and cut, stack, and carry off the wood from the 1929 burned area in the southwest corner of the park; later they cleaned up after the 1936 fires. During their time in the park, they constructed five three-room homes for park employees, prepared 150 acres of campground sites, built fire lookouts, constructed

CCC Camp No. 2 near Apgar at the foot of Lake McDonald.
George Grant, 1933. Courtesy Glacier National Park Archives.

National Park's ranger-in-charge John George "Kootenai" Brown philosophized that wildlife and geology did not recognize borders and that the boundary line that separated Glacier and Waterton national parks should be eliminated.

In 1931 the Rotary Clubs of Alberta, Saskatchewan, British Columbia, and Montana began echoing Brown and Reynolds' campfire philosophy. They agreed that the two national parks were really one wilderness, and some formal recognition of this truth should exist.

There was another and perhaps greater force driving the interest in joining the two parks: the winds of war. When the Rotarians made their proposal in 1931, Adolf Hitler and Germany's Nazi party were on the rise in Europe, and the Japanese had invaded Manchuria in an unde-

Pledge of Peace

Nearly every year since the 1932 dedication, park officials, Rotarians, Blackfeet leaders, and other dignitaries have met at either Waterton or Glacier to commemorate the International Peace Park. In 1947 native-stone cairns were built at the Chief Mountain border crossing. As part of the public dedication of the cairns, the first Hands-Across-the-Border ceremony was held. Those present shook hands and spoke this pledge: "In the name of God, we will not take up arms against each other. We will work for peace, maintain liberty, strive for freedom, and demand equal opportunity for all mankind. May the long-existing peace between our two nations stimulate other people to follow this example. We thank thee, O God."

trails and roads, made improvements to the Going-to-the-Sun Road, and carried in and laid six and a half miles of telephone cable across Logan Pass. Whenever a fire erupted in the park, the "Cs" were called in to help the fire crews.

When the United States entered World War II, all the CCC projects were stopped, and the last camp was evacuated on July 17, 1942. The young men of the CCC left a legacy, and a void, when they marched off to serve in the armed services—or returned to the farm or headed to the cities to work in the factories.

In its nine years, the CCC taught 40,000 illiterate men to read and write and gave thousands more training in a variety of trades. The CCC had become the largest government labor force in U.S. history, employing more than 2.5 million men before the last tent was folded and the men went on to serve in World War II.

A Peace Park

It was an idea hatched as two men sat around a campfire in the early 1900s. Glacier National Park's ranger Albert "Death on the Trail" Reynolds and Waterton

clared war with China. The Rotarians believed that an International Peace Park would promote the continuing goodwill that had existed between Canada and

International Peace Park Ceremony, 1932.
Courtesy Glacier National Park Archives.

Logo for the Waterton–Glacier International Peace Park.

Courtesy Glacier National Park Archives and the superintendents of Glacier National Park and Waterton Lakes National Park.

Two miles east of Logan Pass is the 408-foot-long east-side tunnel, pictured here on July 12, 1933. Mount Clements rises in the background.

George Grant. Courtesy Glacier National Park Archives.

the United States for well over 100 years and would provide a beacon of hope to other nations.

The Rotarians persuaded their government officials to take up the cause in the U.S. Congress and the Canadian Parliament. In May 1932 the dream for Waterton–Glacier International Peace Park became a reality.

On June 18, 1932, Canadian and U.S. officials, Rotarian dignitaries from around the world, and Blackfeet leaders gathered at the Glacier Park Hotel at Midvale (East Glacier) to dedicate the new Waterton–Glacier International Peace Park. They were joined by a troop of Eagle Scouts and a troop of King Scouts, four Canadian Mounted Police officers, and nearly 2,000 citizens from both countries. There were a number of inspiring speeches and songs, as well as the unveiling of a bronze plaque inscribed with the following message: "Permanently commemorating the relationship of Peace and Good-will existing between the peoples and governments of Canada and the United States."

The Going-to-the-Sun Road Crosses the Divide

The National Park Service issued two contracts to speed up construction of the 10.5 miles of the Going-to-the-Sun Road from Logan Pass to the village of St. Mary. The two contractors—A. R. Guthrie and Company of Portland, Oregon, and Colonial Building Company of Spokane, Washington—and

In June, 1932 a gas-powered shovel removes snow from the west side of Logan Pass in order to open the Going-to-the-Sun Road.

Courtesy Glacier National Park Archives.

On the east side of Logan Pass, workers excavate the roadway circa 1932.
Courtesy Glacier National Park Archives.

subcontractor Archie R. Douglas were charged with completing the road by 1933.

The road on the east side of the Continental Divide, which provides a view of some of the park's finest scenery, was not as technically difficult to construct as the road along the Garden Wall on the west side, but it still challenged the best of men. The crews had a variety of difficult situations to overcome—including steep slopes, wicked weather, monstrous snowdrifts, and varied terrain. The most difficult construction on the east side was boring a 408-foot-long tunnel through a steep hillside. The men had to build a trail 200 feet above the road from Logan Pass to above the tunnel site to bring in construction equipment and supplies. Then they shouldered jackhammers, dynamite, ties, drill steel, and other tools needed to bore a hole through the mountain and packed them down a 100-foot drop over a 300-foot switchback, then climbed down another 100 feet on a ladder to a bench that they had previously blasted out of the side of the cliff to create a work platform. The tunnel crews worked in three shifts, boring five feet,

four inches every twenty-four hours. They punched through the wall of rock on October 19, 1931.

Among the many other impressive engineering feats on this portion of the Going-to-the-Sun Road are the retaining walls along the Golden Stairs above St. Mary Lake and the 190-foot rubble stone Baring Bridge across Sunrift Gorge.

The Going-to-the-Sun Road was unofficially opened in 1932, officially opened in 1933, and finally completed in 1934.

Workers remove rock blasted from the future roadway circa 1932.
Courtesy Glacier National Park Archives.

Dedicating the Going-to-the-Sun Road

Their pocketbooks may have been thin, but nothing was going to stop a buoyant crowd of 4,000 Canadians and Americans from gathering at Logan Pass on July 15, 1933. They came by train, private automobile, and jammer bus to attend the dedication of the Going-to-the-Sun Road. The occasion also commemorated the first anniversary of the Waterton–Glacier International Peace Park.

The weather was pleasant, the scenery spectacular, and the drive on the Going-to-the-Sun Road an adventure. Dressed in full regalia, Blackfeet, Salish, and Kootenai tribe members greeted celebrants. There were also a hundred or so young men of the Civilian Conservation Corps who had arrived that summer to work on park trails and roads.

A picnic lunch was served, followed by the formal ceremonies. The program began with the placement of a memorial plaque honoring Stephen Mather for his contribution to all national parks and for his role in creating the Going-to-the-Sun Road.

W. A. Buchanan of the Canadian Parliament chronicled the successes of the Waterton–Glacier International Peace Park's first year and the importance of continuing the strong declarations of peace

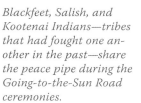

Blackfeet, Salish, and Kootenai Indians—tribes that had fought one another in the past—share the peace pipe during the Going-to-the-Sun Road ceremonies.
George Grant.
Courtesy Glacier National Park Archives.

These may be the first tour buses over Logan Pass on July 15, 1933. The first bus was driven by Aubrey Chapman, the second by Bill Lindsay.
T. J. Hileman.
Courtesy Glacier National Park Archives.

between the two countries. Montana's Senator Burton K. Wheeler spoke about the opening of the road, then turned the podium over to Montana's Governor Frank Cooney. "We may confidently declare that there is no highway which will give the sightseer, the lover of grandeur of the Creator's handiwork, more thrills, more genuine satisfaction deep down in his being than will a trip over this road," he said.

Between elegant speeches, the Blackfeet Tribal Band played music, and a choir from the youthful tenors and baritones of the CCC entertained the crowd.

To the great enjoyment of the spectators, a colorful pageantry of the Blackfeet, Salish, and Kootenai tribes provided the grand finale. Years ago these tribes had been enemies, but their animosity toward one another had dimmed with the passing of time. Now, tribal members, dressed in their ceremonial regalia of beaded buckskin, and the chiefs, wearing full headdress, shared the pipe of peace, then chanted and danced their traditional songs to the ancient beat of drums.

The Blackfeet Tribal Band poses for a photo at the dedication ceremonies.
Courtesy Glacier National Park Archives.

*Ice cave at the foot of the
Boulder Glacier, 1932.*
Courtesy Glacier National Park Archives.

Two cars make their way along the road cut through snowfields along the Garden Wall and Haystack Butte in 1934.
George Grant.
Courtesy Glacier National Park Archives.

A 1930s Great Northern Railway advertisement invites travelers to enjoy Glacier's "broad roads and highways."
Courtesy Glacier National Park Archives.

The "Reds"

Despite the Depression in the 1930s, visitation to Glacier increased when the Going-to-the-Sun Road opened in 1933. The original 1914 buses, however, were not up to the job of carrying passengers up the winding road and over the high passes of the Continental Divide to the east side of the park. It was going to take more powerful engines and better equipped buses to "go to the sun."

Howard Hays, owner of Glacier Park Transportation Company, ordered 18 buses at $5,000 each. They were designed especially for Glacier by Count Alexis de Sakhoffsky, an industrial stylist. F. W. Black, then president of the White Motor Company, and Herman Bender of the Bender Body Company, which supplied the bodies, were also involved in the design of the new buses.

The first buses arrived in 1935, and by 1939 the company was operating thirty-five brand-new, modern buses. They were painted red to match the berries of the mountain ash. These Glacier "reds" had a canvas top that could be rolled back and stored in a rear compartment. Each bus had electric headlamps, which were a great improvement over the 1914 models, which had headlamps illuminated by acetylene gas. The buses also had a door for each seat, instead of just one door for loading all the passengers. A metal rod extending from one side of

Glacier "reds" deliver visitors to the Glacier Park Hotel.
T. J. Hileman.
Courtesy Glacier National Park Archives.

A Great Northern Railway advertisement depicts riders of the roads and trails at Swiftcurrent Lake.
Courtesy John Chase and Burlington Northern–Santa Fe Railway.

and the public was not about to give up their beloved "reds." A grassroots effort turned into strong public and private support for renovating the historic buses. Thanks to Glacier Park, Inc., the National Park Service, the Ford Motor Company, and many private citizens, the fleet of nearly three dozen buses was remounted on chassis that matched the antique bodies and could carry the running gear (motor, transmission, steering, and braking systems). The historic red buses returned to Glacier in 2002 with a slightly modernized look and eco-friendly gasoline/propane bi-fuel systems to again shuttle sightseers up and over the Continental Divide on the Going-to-the-Sun Road.

A Glacier "red" takes passengers past the Weeping Wall.
Courtesy Glacier National Park Archives.

the bus to the other was installed over the seats so that tourists could stand up and hold on while taking photographs as they rode along.

Howard Hays continued operating the red buses until 1957, when he sold the Glacier Park Transportation Company to the Glacier Park Hotel Company. Four years later the buses were turned over to Glacier Park, Inc.

Glacier's 1930s vintage red buses carried visitors up and over the Going-to-the-Sun Road for the next sixty years, racking up 600,000 miles each. They were upgraded with power steering and automatic transmissions in 1989. The bodies were still sound in 1999 but cracks had appeared in the chassis and the buses were taken out of service.

However, the buses had become an icon of Glacier,

Red buses near the Glacier Park Station are ready to take Great Northern Railway passengers through Glacier National Park.
Courtesy John Chase.

Members of the U.S. Air Force stationed at a satellite airfield in Cut Bank, Montana, visit Swiftcurrent for the day. The charred hillside in the background is the result of the 1936 Heavens Peak Fire, which burned portions of the Swiftcurrent Auto Camp and Ranger Station, destroyed most of the Many Glacier chalets, and threatened the Many Glacier Hotel.

9

Making Do in Wartime 1940–1949

O N D ECEMBER 7, 1941—*what President Franklin Roosevelt described as "a date which will live in infamy"—Japanese airplanes swooped out of the sky and bombed Pearl Harbor. Stunned Americans suddenly found themselves at war. Glacier National Park's rangers, guides, cooks, baggage handlers, and gear jammers joined the thousands of young men lined up at recruiting stations around the nation to enlist in the armed services.*

Young women, who worked as waitresses, laundresses, and hotel clerks, also joined the armed services—or followed the example of Rosie the Riveter and worked in the factories building ships, planes, jeeps, and tanks.

As Americans geared up to fight in World War II, visitation to Glacier fell abruptly. Gas, tires, butter, beef, and a host of other goods that were needed for the war effort were rationed. Railroads repurposed their resort trains to move war materials and troops. In 1943 the Great Northern Railway whistled through East and West Glacier without stopping. That same year the Glacier Park Hotel Company closed its hotels, except for Rising Sun/Roes Creek, and by 1944 nearly all the facilities were idle.

Picking up the Slack

Although the park facilities were idle, there was still work to be done, including fires to be fought.

Except for those rangers and other park employees who were either too old or not eligible to join the armed services, there were few men available to take care of the park. During the war years, a cadre of conscientious objectors assigned to Civilian Public Service Camp Number 55 in Belton assisted with park maintenance.

Prior to 1940 men who opposed active military service on religious grounds—such as the Mennonites, the Church of the Brethren, the Amish, the Hutterites, and the Quakers—were still subject to the draft and could be sent into battle. Prompted by representatives of these churches, a bill was passed in 1940 that provided a means for conscientious objectors to serve in an alternative "humanitarian" service. The Civilian Public Service (CPS) program was created from this legislation.

Civilian Public Service Camp Number 55 in Belton opened in September 1942 and operated until

1946. According to Dave Walter in his 2005 book *Rather Than War: The Story of Civilian Public Service Camp Number 55*, more than 550 men served at the Glacier camp. Their only pay was room and board.

The CPS workers performed a variety of jobs. They built park employee homes using prefabricated wooden wall panels taken from the 1930s CCC camps in the park. In winter they helped with snow removal, cut wood for the camp, and hauled wood to the outlying district ranger stations. In the spring and summer the CPS men built and maintained trails, manned and built fire lookouts, fought wildland fires, worked in the sawmill, and maintained phone lines.

In 1945 Daniel J. Headings was one of twenty-four men who built the Heavens Peak Lookout. The lookout was built on solid rock, and the mortar work was the first Headings had ever done, but under the supervision of foreman Steward Swanberg, he and the crew managed to get the job done, and the lookout still stands.

In a 1975 interview Headings related a story of the Japanese phosphorous bombs. During the war the Japanese released balloons carrying incinerating phosphorous bombs over the Pacific Ocean. The balloons floated the weather fronts to the Puget Sound, eastern Washington, and northwestern Montana. As they floated along on the air currents, they would dip

The cover of Dave Walter's 2005 book Rather Than War, *which chronicles the Civilian Public Service in Camp 55 at Belton.*
Courtesy Dave Walter.

Clark Gable visits Glacier National Park before serving in the U.S. Air Force.
Courtesy Glacier National Park Archives.

Smiling soldiers pose in front of the restored Swiftcurrent Auto Camp store circa 1943.
Courtesy John Chase.

The men of the Civilian Public Service built the Heavens Peak Lookout in 1945.
Courtesy Glacier National Park Archives.

Ernie Pyle

Prior to covering World War II, journalist Ernie Pyle frequently hiked in Glacier's backcountry. He described his journey through Glacier in the 1935 edition of Home Country as the "Colossal Pyle Walking Expedition from the United States to the Dominion of Canada." His adventures in Glacier were also published in a 1940 Glacier National Park brochure. Pyle wrote:

When you walk through the Rockies it is not often you can see your trail very far ahead. You approach each bend with the excitement of an explorer, never knowing what vast scene will be revealed. It was around one of these bends that I came upon Ahern Pass and Ahern Snowbank. One minute I was walking along level, on an easy trail across a gentle slope, and the next I was looking down hundreds of feet over sheer cliff. There was really no danger. The trail was six or eight feet wide. You'd have to have St. Vitus's dance to jitter yourself over the side. Yet one cowboy I know, who has ridden every foot of Glacier Park, told me Ahern Ledge scared him worse than any other place in the park. The first time he crossed it, he was riding a horse that was blind in one eye. It happened to be the outside eye, and the cowboy said that horse tried to see how close to the edge he could walk.

Pyle hiked the fifty miles from Logan Pass to the little village of Waterton Lakes in Alberta in four days and nights. He averaged a "sizzling speed of two miles an hour" and arrived with one Hershey bar left over and without a single blister on his heels.

Declaring his trek a complete success, Pyle wrote, "Our brilliant crossing of the Rockies into this charming land was due solely to the fine spirit of co-operation and sacrifice on the part of my two legs. Without those legs, we would never have got here."

He walked into a "rustic little hotel at Waterton Lakes with my pack on my back. The lady at the desk was very British. I knew she would be impressed when she found how far I had walked. She would be proud to have me aboard, sir, I knew. So I registered smugly, and didn't say a word, just letting my dusty overalls and my tanned and weary countenance spray their full import upon her. She looked at the register card. 'Oh,' she said eagerly, 'did you walk from Washington D.C.?'"

While writing about his adventures in Glacier, Ernie Pyle related a conversation with Viola Marti, the cook at the Fifty Mountain Tent Camp who told

fortunes by examining coffee grounds: "She told me that I didn't take long hikes because I enjoyed the physical sensation of walking, but because I like to be alone. And that was true. She said that as I walked I did a great deal of daydreaming. That was right too, I guess, for when I walk alone I am quite a hero. Oh, I win auto races, and have movie actresses after me, and come back from the wars very sad-looking and with one arm shot off and my column runs in seven hundred papers, and even the savages in darkest Africa know who I am. And out there on Ahern Pass there hadn't been a soul to tell me I was a damn liar."

During World War II, Ernie Pyle became America's most beloved war correspondent, telling the story of war from the soldiers' point of view. He reported from Europe, Africa, and the Pacific, receiving a Pulitzer Prize in 1944 for his work.

On April 18, 1945, on an island off Okinawa Honto, Ernie Pyle was killed by enemy gunfire.

Famed war correspondent Ernie Pyle journeyed across Glacier on foot in 1935, and his story was later featured in this Great Northern Railway brochure.
Courtesy Kintla Archives, Ted Patten and Burlington Northern–Santa Fe Railway.

down, release an incinerating phosphorous bomb, and then rise up sharply as a result of the unloading. The bombs would start a fire when they landed. The U.S. government did not publicize the balloons or the damage they caused. Headings said, "We didn't want the Japanese to know of their effectiveness, and it seemed to work, because the enemy discontinued using them after a while." Park employees and CPS workers were told to be alert and report them right away; they were not to touch them or talk about them. Headings spotted the first one that dropped into Glacier and reported it immediately. The Army roped off the area, and he never heard anything more about the incident.

Welcome Back
When World War II ended, the nation was eager to shed its wartime worries and have some fun again.

Glacier National Park reopened on June 15, 1946, and the Great Northern Railway's luxury passenger trains, the *Oriental Limited* and the *Empire Builder,* once again brought vacationers to Glacier. The hotels and the chalets—except St. Mary, Going-to-the-Sun, and Cut Bank, which had been torn down—reopened. Horses were saddled and ready to ride the trails. Boats returned to the lakes; automobiles and the red buses loaded with carefree sightseers hummed their way up the Going-to-the-Sun Road. More than 200,000 visitors came to Glacier in 1946 and the numbers increased every year.

Another Kind of Battle
In 1944 and 1945, while war raged in Europe and the Pacific, another kind of battle brewed on the homefront. It would not be the first nor the last battle the

The Great Northern Railway goat welcomes visitors back to Glacier National Park after World War II "for folks who've craved for an eyeful of the most eye-filling country in the U.S.A."

Courtesy John Chase and Burlington Northern–Santa Fe Railway.

National Park Service and the public would fight to preserve Glacier National Park.

As part of the development of the Columbia River Basin for increased water power, the Department of Defense Army Corps of Engineers and the Bonneville Power Administration proposed building a dam on the North Fork of the Flathead River near Glacier View Mountain and flood thousands of acres in the northwestern part of the park. In 1948 the discussion reached the national level and by 1949 Secretary of Defense James Forrestal and Secretary of the Interior Julius Krug stepped in. They agreed that the dam would not be built without the full agreement of both departments. The two departments never agreed, and the threat of the Glacier View Dam was stopped.

Museums and the Glacier Natural History Association

"No place is a place until the things that have happened in it are remembered in history, ballads, yarns, legends, or monuments."

—from A Sense of Place by Wallace Stegner

Glacier Natural History Association

The forerunner organization providing "a sense of place" for Glacier visitors began in 1926, when a group of naturalists and park rangers formed the Glacier National Park Museum Society. Morton J. Elrod, a professor at the University of Montana and a seasonal naturalist at the park, was president, and renowned conservationist George Bird Grinnell was honorary president. The work and fate of the society is not clear. It appears its intended purpose was absorbed by the park service in 1929, when George C. Ruhle was assigned as Glacier's chief naturalist. He began comprehensive interpretive programs and collected historic artifacts, documents, and wildlife specimens to document the park's history and resources to support his educational and scientific programs.

Ruhle also planned a series of small museums throughout the park. In 1932 a tent museum was set up at Many Glacier. In 1935 the museum displays were moved to the dorm lobby. The dorm and museum displays burned in 1936. Due to limits in funding, plans for the series of small museums stalled.

Currently, the park's museum and archives collection are located at the park's headquarters; researchers and the general public may use the facilities by appointment.

In 1941 the Glacier Natural History Association (GNHA) was formed to supplement the park's museum and interpretive program. The association mirrored the nation's first natural history association organized in the 1920s at Yosemite National Park. GNHA serves as a partner to the park to bring together collections of Glacier's scientific and natural history materials "for the instruction, entertainment and education of park visitors." The association was incorporated in 1946 as a nonprofit scientific and historical organization engaged in educational work for the park. Since the 1940s GNHA has expanded its role to include sponsoring experimental programs and research, including the Native America Speaks and Artists in Residence programs.

A bear known as Gertie and her two cubs look for a handout in this iconic 1958 photograph by Pulitzer Prize–winning photographer Mel Ruder of the Hungry Horse News.
Mel Ruder.
Courtesy Patsi Morton and Glacier National Park Archives.

10

Making Up for Lost Time
1950–1959

I N T H E P R O S P E R O U S 1 9 5 0 S *Americans were determined to enjoy themselves and make up for time lost during World War II. They embraced suburban living, television, rock and roll, and outdoor recreation with gusto. Visiting national parks and experiencing wilderness were high on their list of vacation priorities.*

Glacier National Park became even more popular with the American public when it was chosen as a backdrop for several Hollywood films and was featured in song and print.

A movement to revive Indian culture began, and visitors enjoyed the first annual North American Indian Days Celebration on the Blackfeet Reservation that borders the park.

By 1954 visitation to Glacier National Park had tripled since its record 1946 year of 200,000 visitors, and park officials were predicting even greater numbers in the coming decade. They knew they had to be ready.

Glacier in Pop Culture

The Great Northern Railway had been crafting sophisticated ads to draw tourists to Glacier National Park and the surrounding area since the 1890s. In the 1950s they again produced a variety of print ads to appeal to the post-war mentality of modern families, who were eager to shed their worries and have fun. Ads touted Glacier as the "Land of the Shining Moun-

tains" and promised never a dull day in the "Land of a Thousand Thrills." Enticed travelers flocked to the park—but increasingly by auto instead of by train, much to the chagrin of the Great Northern Railway.

Glacier also starred in several feature films, including *Dangerous Mission* and *Cattle Queen of Montana*. Movie stars touring the park while making films upstaged even the grizzlies. Tourists lined up to get autographs when they spotted Victor Mature, Piper Lauri, Barbara Stanwyck, Gary Cooper, or Ronald Reagan enjoying the sights in Glacier's shining mountains.

North American Indian Days

The Blackfeet have a long tradition of large gatherings and celebrations—traditionally to trade goods or reunite with family members. In 1951 Glacier National Park's neighbors, the Blackfeet Tribal Council, sponsored the first annual North American Indian Days Celebration in Browning, Montana. Tribes from the northwestern states and Canada gathered to drum and dance, much as their ancestors did. The celebration was the beginning of a movement to revive the Blackfeet culture and heritage that would only grow in the coming decades.

Mission 66

Throughout the country, national parks were wrestling with the demands that increased visitation was having on park roads and facilities. What worried park officials even more was what was predicted to come: an estimated 80 million visitors to national parks annually by the mid-sixties.

In 1955 Conrad Wirth, the director of the National Park Service, proposed a ten-year building plan to "regenerate and modernize" the national parks. It was the largest park improvement program ever initiated by the National Park Service. The proposed date for completion was 1966—to coincide with the fiftieth anniversary of the National Park Service and to accommodate the expected 80 million national park visitors that year. With 1966 as the goal year, the program was titled Mission 66.

Mission 66 met with immediate criticism from preservationists, who argued that the program was incompatible with the National Park Service's role of preserving and protecting the lands in their wilderness state. "To popularize and commercialize the national parks is to cheapen them and reduce them to the level of ordinary playgrounds," wrote Devereaux Butcher, executive secretary and field representative for the National Park Association. To preservation-minded men such as Butcher, the Mission 66 program attracted people to the parks for the wrong reasons. The increased development in the parks appealed to those who liked to be entertained in comfort and come to the parks "not from any compulsion or love or interest, but from idleness or

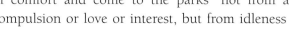

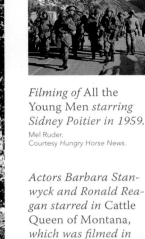

Filming of All the Young Men *starring Sidney Poitier in 1959.*
Mel Ruder.
Courtesy Hungry Horse News.

Actors Barbara Stanwyck and Ronald Reagan starred in Cattle Queen of Montana, *which was filmed in the St. Mary Valley of Glacier National Park in 1954.*
Mel Ruder, 1954.
Courtesy Patsi Morton and Glacier National Park Archives.

Unknown Blackfeet child at the North American Indian Days Celebration. Her shell-decorated dress and 1950s saddle shoes unintentionally combine the old with the new.
Courtesy John Chase.

Glacier Park Waltz

Clarence Cunningham's song "The Glacier Park Waltz" reminded visitors that Glacier was a "majestic land of peace and harmony." Rock and roll defined the 1950s, yet this ballad became popular in the park and surrounding communities.

vapid curiosity; not for inspiration but for thrills."

It was symbolic of the decade that the concerns of the preservationists did not stop Mission 66. Their ideals, however, would catch on in the next decade and guide the development of Glacier National Park

In 1954 the once weekly ranger-led trips to Grinnell Glacier became daily events to accommodate the increased number of visitors.
Mel Ruder, 1957.
Courtesy Patsi Morton and Glacier National Park Archives.

for years to come.

Mission 66 introduced two major changes to national parks: the concept of "visitor centers" to replace the decentralized park villages and a modern style of architecture for park buildings.

The visitor centers were envisioned as the hub of the park interpretive programs, helping visitors understand the meaning of the park and its features, and

Visitors gather to take in the snow-covered view at Logan Pass.
Courtesy Tom Mulvaney.

Traffic comes to a halt as curious onlookers spot triplet bear cubs crossing a Glacier National Park road.
Mel Ruder, 1951.
Courtesy Patsi Morton and Glacier National Park Archives.

An early winter view of Lake McDonald.
Mel Ruder.
Courtesy Patsi Morton and Glacier National Park Archives.

Skiers enjoy the warm summer sun at Logan Pass.
Mel Ruder.
Courtesy *Hungry Horse News.*

The perfect spot for a photograph. Children pose for their mother in a Glacier National Park lake in 1958.
Mel Ruder, 1958.
Courtesy Patsi Morton and Glacier National Park Archives.

Clearing snow from the Going-to-the-Sun Road near the Garden Wall on April 18, 1952.
Mel Ruder.
Courtesy Patsi Morton and Glacier National Park Archives.

how best to protect, use, and appreciate them. The centers would have exhibit space, auditoriums for films and presentations, information desks, and administrative offices and restrooms. The centers were eventually expanded to include retail book sales and gift shops.

Three visitor centers were planned for Glacier: one at the summit of the Going-to-the-Sun Road

and one near each of the two park entrances. Two were completed, but the third, at Apgar, was never built. Plans are currently in the works to develop the Apgar Visitor Center by 2016, in time for the centennial of the National Park Service.

In addition to visitor centers, Mission 66 provided for the construction of the coffee shop and grill at Lake McDonald Lodge, the restaurant at Rising Sun, the ranger station at Goat Haunt, housing for park employees, and new utility and maintenance buildings in the park headquarters area in West Glacier. The program also expanded campgrounds and parking areas and added turnouts along the Going-to-the-Sun Road.

Visitors take in the glorious views from atop Logan Pass in June 1950.

Mel Ruder, 1950.
Courtesy Patsi Morton and
Glacier National Park Archives.

Logan Pass Visitor Center.

Mel Ruder.
Courtesy Patsi Morton and
Glacier National Park Archives.

Naturalist George Ruhle finds the perfect vista point to view Jonah's Bowl and Pitamakan Lake in 1952.

Mel Ruder.
Courtesy Hungry Horse News.

In August 1967 the Garden Wall Fire roared through Glacier National Park.

Mel Ruder
Courtesy Patsi Morton and
Glacier National Park Archives.

11

Challenge, Change, and Tragedy
1960–1969

A S T H E 1 9 6 0 S D A W N E D, *newly elected President John F. Kennedy promised the nation would enter a New Frontier— explore uncharted areas of science and space, solve conflicts between nations, and challenge pockets of ignorance and prejudice. The decade was marked by the assassinations of President Kennedy in 1963 and Civil Rights leader Dr. Martin Luther King, Jr., in 1968. The 1960s also saw the first man on the moon, the creation of the Peace Corp, and the escalation of the war in Vietnam.*

Glacier National Park ushered in the decade with a joyous celebration of its golden anniversary. The excitement was soon followed by changes in hotel management, unprecedented numbers of park visitors, Mission 66 construction, floods, grizzly attacks, and forest fires. The 1960s were a decade of change that would permanently impact the park.

The Great Northern Railway Bows Out

After nearly seventy years of hands-on influence and investment in the development and management of Glacier National Park, the Great Northern Railway decided to bow out. Despite a steady increase in visitation since the end of World War II, Glacier's hotels were struggling. Only about fourteen percent of visitors were staying in hotels; the majority opted to camp or rent rustic cabins.

In 1951 the Great Northern Railway decided to sell its Glacier National Park properties. The company that had created a tourist mecca out of raw wilderness, constructed or financed many of Glacier's early roads and trails, and arranged for most of the boating, trail riding, and mountaineering activities decided it was time to concentrate solely on the railroad business.

In 1960 the Great Northern Railway found a buyer and sold all its holdings in the park to Don Hummel, an Arizona businessman who had previously operated facilities in Mount McKinley and Lassen Volcanic national parks. Hummel operated the business as Glacier Park, Inc. under a twenty-five-year contract with the National Park Service. In 1981 Hummel sold Glacier Park, Inc. to Greyhound Food Management of Phoenix, Arizona. Over the years the hotels and chalets lost some of their historic elegance to the modern ideas and methods of hotel management.

(Far left) Glacier National Park hosted the National Governors' Conference in 1960, the park's fiftieth year.
Courtesy John Chase.

(Left) Great Northern Railway ad announcing Glacier National Park's fiftieth anniversary.
Courtesy John Chase and Burlington Northern–Santa Fe Railway.

A bulldozer plummeted 350 feet off the Going-to-the-Sun Road after a mass of snow gave way in June 1964.
Mel Ruder.
Courtesy Hungry Horse News.

General Motors donated 200 cars for use at the National Governors' Conference, hosted by Glacier National Park in 1960.
Mel Ruder.
Courtesy Patsi Morton and Glacier National Park Archives.

Various postcards depicting the Glacier National Park of the 1960s.
Courtesy Tom Mulvaney.

Along the southern border of Glacier, the raging waters of the Middle Fork of the Flathead River washed out miles of the Great Northern Railway mainline and U.S. Highway 2 roadbeds, leaving sections of track suspended in midair, eroding slopes, and leaving telephone poles dangling, held up only by their wires. Shown below is the flooded 21-foot-high tunnel extension of the Great Northern mainline 2.5 miles east of West Glacier.
Mel Ruder.
Courtesy Patsi Morton and
Glacier National Park Archives.

The small village of St. Mary near the eastern entrance of Glacier National Park was evacuated when three feet of water flowed through the streets, flooding homes and businesses, knocking out electrical lines, contaminating the water supply, and leaving layers of mud and debris in its wake.
Courtesy of Montana Historical
Society, Helena, Montana.

The Great Flood of 1964

It was a storm that would go down in the history books. In June 1964 a renegade mass of moist air from the Gulf of Mexico moved over the western plains and the Continental Divide, mixed with the cooler air over the mountains, and created a lee-side storm on the normally wind-sheltered slopes of the Rocky Mountains.

The snowpack in the mountains in the winter of 1963–1964 had been less than normal. In April and May, however, heavy snowfall blanketed the mountains, creating a record snowpack. When the moist air mass from the Gulf rolled in, flood conditions were perfect.

The rains started as a soft drizzle—then became a torrent. During the first twenty-four hours, ten inches of rain fell at Lake McDonald, and more than eight inches fell in Browning, east of the park. The Flathead, Sun, and Marias rivers flooded, as did parts of the Missouri and Teton rivers. The Sun River flooded the western end of Great Falls to the rooftops. Towns in Cascade, Chouteau, Teton, Pondera, and Toole

counties, as well as the towns in the Flathead Valley, were all hit hard.

According to Aaron Parrett in his 2004 article titled "Montana's Worst Natural Disaster," in *Montana: The Magazine of Western History,* the worst of the damage occurred on the Blackfeet Reservation, where "raging rivers destroyed 265 homes, 20,000 acres of farmland along the creeks, two large dams…irrigation facilities on which 37,000 acres of cropland depended, barns, corrals, sheds and livestock, all bridges and much of the Reservation road system."

President Lyndon Johnson declared nine of Montana's counties a federal disaster area on June 11, 1964. When the storm passed and the waters subsided, 30 people were reported drowned, 100 were missing, and more than 1,200 were left homeless.

In Glacier the floodwaters tore out sections of road,

washed away numerous bridges, devastated miles of backcountry trails, destroyed the old Waterton Ranger Station, and flooded sections of several hotels.

The waters of the winding Two Medicine River overflowed its banks, joined the floodwaters of the broken Swift Dam, and created a river two miles wide. It inundated farmlands, washing away houses and livestock.

The raging waters of the Middle Fork of the Flathead River mangled the Great Northern Railway's main line west of Summit and ate away U.S. Highway 2, blocking all traffic over Marias Pass. The river twisted and fractured the bridge into the park at West Glacier and tore the concrete superstructure off the historic 1920 Belton Bridge, isolating the park headquarters and area residents until an NPS contractor repaired the Belton Bridge three weeks later.

The deluge running through the Swiftcurrent Valley washed out the only road to Many Glacier, flooded the hotel, and cut the area off from the rest of the world for eight days.

Snyder Creek swelled, spilling over its banks, and Lake McDonald peaked at eight feet above its normal high level. Floodwaters ruined portions of the Lake

An avalanche of rock, gravel, uprooted trees, and debris washed out sections of the Going-to-the-Sun Road between McDonald Creek and the Garden Wall.
Courtesy Glacier National Park Archives.

Upstream of the West Glacier Bridge, the raging waters destroyed all but the arch of the Belton Bridge, constructed in 1920. A timber-trestle superstructure was hastily placed on the arch to provide temporary access to the park while the West Glacier Bridge was being replaced.
J. Mohlenrich, 1964.
Courtesy Glacier National Park.

During the flood of 1964, the rampaging Middle Fork of the Flathead River twisted and fractured the 1938 West Glacier Bridge and rather neatly inserted logs into the structure. The damaged bridge was torn down and replaced by a steel bridge in 1965.
Wasem, 1964.
Courtesy Glacier National Park Archives.

The wind-whipped Glacier Wall Fire leaps across McDonald Creek and the Going-to-the-Sun Road and races up the Garden Wall in August 1967.
Mel Ruder.
Courtesy Patsi Morton and
Glacier National Park Archives.

Sightseers watch as the lightning-ignited Glacier Wall Fire runs up the mountainside.
Mel Ruder.
Courtesy *Hungry Horse News.*

McDonald Lodge dining room and completely destroyed the footbridge that crossed the creek.

Flood damage to the Going-to-the-Sun Road was estimated at $2.25 million. The destruction was particularly heavy along upper McDonald Creek, requiring some sections of the road to be completely reconstructed in 1965.

Superintendent Keith Neilson, his staff, and park employees and contractors worked around the clock to reopen the park in record time. Emergency work projects were initiated to rebuild and replace the damaged facilities and repair park roads and bridges. The damage to some backcountry bridges and large sections of trail was considered too expensive to restore, and they were abandoned.

The Glacier Wall Fire

In August 1967, three years after the devastating floods, lightning from a storm ignited twenty fires in the park. They roared up the mountains and through the steep terrain of the Continental Divide. Along the Going-to-the-Sun Road sixty-mile-per-hour winds drove the fires across McDonald Creek and up the precipitous cliffs of the Garden Wall. Park firefighters fought the raging blazes as long as they could without help. Finally firefighters from around the West, including Alaska, were brought in. Nearly 3,500 men

Grizzly bears.
Courtesy Glacier National Park Archives.

worked through August and September to bring the fires under control. More than 6,500 acres burned that summer.

Night of the Grizzlies
"Roy felt something bite deeply into his right shoulder and scrape against the bone, and with a tremendous exercise of his will, he neither cried out nor moved. The biting stopped, and Roy opened his eyes long enough to make out the shadow of a bear standing

The National Park Service uses culvert-style traps to capture and transport nuisance bears. The bears are usually relocated to distant wilderness areas.
Mel Ruder.
Courtesy Hungry Horse News.

on all fours above the helpless girl and tearing at her body," wrote Jack Olsen, author of *Night of the Grizzlies,* a 1969 book that details one terrible night in Glacier National Park.

On August 13, 1967, two grizzly bears attacked two different groups of backcountry campers separated by some ten miles of mountains and valleys. At the Granite Park campground near the Granite Park Chalet, nineteen-year-old Julie Helgeson was killed and partially consumed by a grizzly, and her companion Roy Ducat was mauled. Ten miles away at the Trout Lake campsite, another nineteen-year-old—Michele Koons, who worked summers at the Lake McDonald Lodge gift shop—was mauled in her sleeping bag. Her arm was ripped off and she was dragged up a hill. She died before rescue crews could take her out of the mountains. The bears were quickly hunted by park rangers and killed.

Julie Helgeson and Michele Koons were the first people ever killed by grizzlies in Glacier National Park. The fact the deaths occurred in a single night drew national attention to Glacier.

Speculation in newspapers and among park employees and visitors on what caused the bears to at-

Although feeding bears garbage was against park policy, it had been common practice in Glacier and other parks since the 1800s. The tragic grizzly attacks in 1967 forced officials to reduce bear–human confrontations by enforcing the policy and launching an aggressive program to encourage backcountry users to pack items out that were packed in.
Courtesy Glacier National Park Archives.

A young black bear growls at photographers from atop a garbage can near a Glacier campground.
Mel Ruder.
Courtesy Patsi Morton and Glacier National Park Archives.

tack and kill the women ranged from "the bears were drunk on overripe huckleberries" to "the victims had not followed established backcountry procedures and invited disaster." Critics of the National Park Service claimed that shoddy backcountry management allowed employees at Granite Park to invite bears to come near the chalet for the viewing enjoyment of guests by dumping garbage; this was against park policy, but it was not aggressively enforced at the time. Bears had been feeding on garbage in Glacier since the late 1800s, and they had never killed a human in the history of the park. No one believed they ever would.

Jack Olsen, in his quest to find out why the attacks occurred after six decades of relatively peaceful coexistence, concluded simply that it was inevitable: "By 1967, man with his hated smell and his bumbling manner was pushing harder and harder on the grizzly." Almost one million visitors had come to the park that summer and "a goodly number of them were taking to the

A ranger leads hikers up the Garden Wall Trail, later named the Highline Trail, in 1962.
Mel Ruder.
Courtesy Patsi Morton and Glacier National Park Archives.

beautiful trails that led straight into the domain of the grizzly and camping out in areas the bears considered their own." It had been a hot summer and the bears' favorite food—the berry crop—was lean. Olsen argued that the bears were hungry, crowded, and angry, and it was no wonder someone was killed.

The park launched an aggressive program to reduce bear-human confrontations. They strictly enforced the rule about not dumping garbage, closed trails where bears were feeding, and expanded public awareness programs on how to avoid contact with bears while camping and hiking.

In spring, snowmelt feeds fast-moving creeks and brings about a profusion of color in Glacier's verdant meadows.
Photo by Tony Bynum.

12

Minding Nature
1970–1979

THE 1970S WERE MARKED *by a continued shift toward conservation—though not always by choice. Americans were asked to slow down to 55 miles per hour to conserve fuel in 1973 when the Organization of Petroleum Countries (OPEC) cut off all oil exports to the United States to protest U.S. support of Israel. In 1974 the embargo was lifted, and motorists once again zipped along on the highways. U.S. troops that had been fighting against communism in Vietnam since 1959 were pulled out by Congress in 1975.*

The United States celebrated its 200th birthday on July 4, 1976, and the environmental movement that started in the 1960s showed it had teeth.

The 1970s set a new course for the future of Glacier National Park. The decade rode in on the winds of the environmental conscience and the legislative atmosphere that had passed the Wilderness Act in the 1960s. Issues such as environmental research and ecosystem preservation came to the forefront. Glacier's backcountry became a research lab for the world. Snowmobiles were banned, controversy erupted over the Logan Pass boardwalk, the grizzlies behaved, and Glacier stretched its borders a bit.

Tourism Takes a Back Seat

Until the 1970s Glacier National Park had been developed and managed for scenic preservation and public use—as were all national parks. Stephen Mather, the first director of the National Park Service, had set the course in 1916 on the premise that the survival of national parks depended on attracting people to visit them, which would then generate continuing public, congressional, and financial support. Mather's premise still rang true, but the people flocking to the national parks after the 1960s were more conservation minded than the generations before them. They were interested in experiencing the wilderness in its pristine state.

The effects of the 1964 Wilderness Act, the 1970 National Environmental Policy Act, and the 1973 Endangered Species Act—as well as the rising concerns of ecologists, wildlife biologists, and preservationists—collided with the National Park Service's sixty years of management practice. The "use and enjoyment" portion of their mandate suddenly became secondary to leaving the wilderness "unimpaired for the enjoyment of future generations."

Nearly all those who visit Glacier National Park stop at Logan Pass to take in the breathtaking scenery, browse the visitor center, or hike the Hidden Lake Trail. The full parking lot in this August 7, 1979, photograph is typical of a summer day in Glacier.
Mel Ruder.
Courtesy Patsi Morton and
Glacier National Park Archives.

Visitors travel the boardwalk between the Logan Pass Visitor Center and Hidden Lake.
Courtesy Glacier National Park Archives.

Construction of the Hidden Lake boardwalk at Logan Pass. One of the most controversial issues about the boardwalk was the initial use of Penta-treated lumber. This wood was subsequently removed from the partially constructed walk.
Courtesy Glacier National Park Archives.

For the Enjoyment of Future Generations
One of the first things park officials did to reduce the impact visitors had on the wilderness was to encourage them to use the permanently developed areas of the park, such as the lodges and the Going-to-the-Sun Road. The park subsidized bus service from Lake McDonald to Logan Pass to help reduce traffic on the Going-to-the-Sun Road. Loop C of Avalanche Campground was closed to restore vegetation and avoid further degradation, and rather than build more campgrounds to accommodate the growing number of summer campers, the park encouraged local businesses to develop campgrounds outside of the park.

In 1971 park managers counted as many as 400

A mountain goat looks out over Lake Ellen Wilson, 1971.
Mel Ruder.
Courtesy Patsi Morton and Glacier National Park Archives.

life in the winter, bringing about weight loss and an increased susceptibility to disease. He also argued that the noise of snowmobiles altered the wilderness experience for snowshoers and skiers.

Turning Back the Clock

Ask any longtime Glacier National Park ranger or park employee about what has changed the most in the park since the 1960s, and the universal response is "wilderness management."

In the past the National Park Service tended to measure its success by the degree to which national park wilderness was left undeveloped and unoccupied. As early as the 1930s, biologists disagreed with the National Park Service position. They challenged the assumption on scientific terms, pointing out that although the backcountry was left undeveloped, the natural conditions were being manipulated by nurturing favored species, such as bears and bighorn sheep, and removing predators, such as wolves and mountain lions; by introducing non-native game fish

Bald eagle.
J. Mohlenrich.
Courtesy Glacier National Park Archives.

Swollen with snowmelt, Baring Creek rushes through rocky terrain. Going-to-the-Sun Mountain catches some late-afternoon sunlight in the background.
©chuckhaney.com.

people per hour hiking from the summit of Logan Pass to Hidden Lake. Certain that number would only increase, they built a 3,700-foot-long boardwalk over the trail to keep hikers from leaving the path, thus protecting the fragile alpine flora. Critics thought it unsightly, charging that it was "undue artificiality in a natural setting." The park argued that preserving the flora along the trail outweighed other concerns, and the boardwalk remained.

Glacier National Park's Superintendent Phillip Iverson took additional conservation steps in 1975 by banning snowmobiles in the park. Iverson reasoned that the noise from the vehicles caused stress on wild-

park policy for the next forty years and beyond. Rangers would continuously be caught up in the struggle to accommodate the public, control record-setting crowds, and preserve the backcountry and its wildlife as though the first non-Indian had never stepped foot in the Glacier wilderness.

To turn back the clock to the early 1800s, the park added a new backcountry ranger to the two existing districts in order to give more attention to preservation activities. Fishing policies were changed: Rangers no longer planted fish to encourage certain species for sports fishermen as they had been doing since the

Bighorn sheep.
Courtesy Randy Smith, Missoula, Montana.

into the rivers and streams; and by suppressing forest fires.

The 1964 Wilderness Act and a 1968 National Park Service policy set the stage for decades of change in park management. The new policy would restore all national parks to "a reasonable illusion of primitive America." The weighty task ahead was not only to prevent future development but to turn the Glacier National Park clock back to the time of the Lewis and Clark Expedition. The directives would dominate

Mountain goat kid.
Photo by Tony Bynum.

Wolf.
S. Cassidy.
Courtesy Glacier National Park Archives.

A couple enjoys the elegant and powerful cascading St. Mary Falls.
Mel Ruder.
Courtesy Patsi Morton and
Glacier National Park Archives.

1920s. Wildlife species were no longer managed, and wolves and mountain lions returned to Glacier. Some trails were abandoned and bridges were removed. Hikers were encouraged to adopt a "leave no trace" backcountry use ethic.

Getting Scientific

Despite the conservation sins of the past, Glacier emerged as a laboratory where scientists could study the relationship between humans and the environ-ment. In 1976 Glacier National Park became a bio-sphere reserve. In 1979 Waterton Lakes National Park also become a biosphere reserve. The joining biosphere reserves are managed as a trans-boundary reserve.

Biosphere reserves throughout the world are intact ecosystems set aside for preservation and study. The designation is given by the United Nations Educa-tional, Scientific, and Cultural Organization under its Man and the Biosphere program, which was started in 1970.

Glacier's designation as a biosphere reserve served as recognition of its value to the world as a biologically diverse ecosystem and emphasized its importance to science and research in promoting a sustained relationship between humans and the Earth.

Glacier Grows a Little

In 1971, the same year the controversial boardwalk was built at Logan Pass and park officials were initiating a series of conservation efforts, Glacier stretched its borders by 233 acres. The Burlington Northern–Santa Fe Railway—the successor to the Great Northern Railway, which had laid tracks along the park's southern border—had eliminated some curves in the line over a period of years and freed up land that was a natural extension of Glacier. The railroad traded a few hundred acres of its land for a few dozen acres of Glacier National Park.

Jim Thompson of the Rocky Mountain Region of the National Park Service and Cliff Martinka of Glacier National Park unveiling the Man and the Biosphere plaque at Logan Pass.
Courtesy Glacier National Park Archives.

In the 1970s the park educated visitors on the impact of people on the wilderness in a series of naturalist-led Eco-Treks.
Courtesy Glacier National Park Archives.

College students from Minnesota come face to face with Glacier's iconic animal, the mountain goat.
Mel Ruder.
Courtesy *Hungry Horse News*.

GOING · TO · THE · SUN

GLACIER NATIONAL PARK

BIKECENTENNIAL

BIKECENTENNIAL   THE NON-PROFIT SERVICE ORGANIZATION FOR RECREATIONAL BICYCLISTS • P.O. BOX 8308, MISSOULA, MONTANA 59807 (406) 721-1776

Poster celebrating the gorgeous views from the Going-to-the-Sun Road.

Monte Dolack, 1987.
www.montedolack.com.

13

A Hodgepodge of Happenings
1980 – 1989

T HE 1980S SAW RONALD REAGAN *ride out of Hollywood west-erns to become president of the United States, the first woman appointed to the Supreme Court, the Berlin Wall crumble, and the explosion of the space shuttle* Challenger. *Wheelers, dealers, and yuppies were getting rich while the sun shone in urban America. In the West, nature went a little berserk: Mount Saint Helens blew its top, a San Francisco earthquake collapsed the Bay Bridge, and forest fires blackened nearly 800,000 acres of Yellowstone National Park.*

For Glacier National Park, the 1980s were a hodgepodge of events and activities. The park celebrated its past and made promises for the future, invited Native Americans back to Glacier, spiffed up the hotels and transportation services, and reached out to visitors with a variety of cultural awareness and nature programs.

Celebrating the Past

The 1980s marked the centennials for several historic events: geologist Raphael Pumpelly and mountain man Hugh Monroe's historic trip through what is now Glacier National Park in 1882; John F. Stevens' discovery of Marias Pass for the Great Northern Railway in 1889, which brought tracks, trains, and tourists to the region; the launch of George Bird Grinnell's efforts to preserve Glacier as a national park; and Montana statehood in 1889.

It also marked fiftieth anniversaries of the establishment of the Waterton–Glacier International Peace Park in 1932 and the completion of the Going-to-the-Sun Road in 1934. In 1985 the Sun Road was designated a National Historic Civil Engineering Landmark.

Promising Peace and Friendship

The idea to annually celebrate the peace and friendship of the United States and Canada was conceived during a summer blizzard atop Logan Pass.

In 1985 the superintendents of Waterton Lakes and Glacier national parks invited various Canadian and American dignitaries and journalists on a hike. The hike offered officials the opportunity to meet and share ideas while exploring the magnificent mountains of the two national parks, and it became an annual superintendent's event.

The first Peace and Friendship Days celebration at Goat Haunt in Glacier National Park in 1987. Glacier National Park's Superintendent Gil Lusk is seated in the front row, far left.
1987.
Courtesy Glacier National Park Archives.

Children ages six to twelve can participate in Glacier's Junior Ranger program.
Courtesy Glacier National Park Archives.

The hikers were at Granite Park when an August blizzard forced them to hike to Logan Pass to board a bus for Lake McDonald and take refuge in a cabin. "We swapped lies about the history of our two countries," reported Blaine Thacker, the Lethbridge Foothills member of the Canadian Parliament who was among the hiking superintendents. While telling stories, the snowed-in hikers came up with the idea to set aside the two days between Canada Day (July 1) and Independence Day (July 4) to recognize and reinforce the peace and friendship of the two countries.

The first Peace and Friendship Days celebration was held in 1987 at the Belly River Campground in Waterton Lakes National Park about two miles north of the U.S./Canada customs stations on Chief Mountain Highway. The location of the event alternates between the two nations each year. Rotary International is an honorary sponsor of this special occasion, and many public and private organizations in both countries gather each year to celebrate the peace between the two nations. The event includes meetings and special guest speakers to further enhance the friendship, goodwill, and shared values of the Waterton–Glacier International Peace Park.

A mountain goat, the unofficial symbol of Glacier National Park and its regal wildness.
Monte Dolack, 1983.
www.montedolack.com.

Teeter-Tottering Tourism Trends

Providing public access and services while also preserving Glacier in its natural state is a perpetual balancing act. Focus on one or the other tends to shift

Park visitors enjoy a ranger talk at the skirt of a snowfield.
Courtesy Glacier National Park Archives.

Granite Park Chalet, constructed of stone quarried from the building site, is a mountain refuge accessible only by trail. Heavens Peak appears in the background.
Courtesy Glacier National Park Archives.

depending on the values and resources of the times.

In the 1970s the park launched vigorous programs to achieve the preservation goals set by the environmental laws of the 1960s and the 1968 National Park Service policy to restore the park to a "reasonable illusion of primitive America." Consumed by preserva-

tion activities, park officials had little time to oversee the activities of the concessionaires that operated the hotels, chalets, and park transportation. At the same time the concessionaires, hampered by runaway inflation in the 1970s and economic recession of the early 1980s, reduced their services, and the condition of the buildings and equipment fell into disrepair.

In the 1980s the preservation programs were making progress, so Gil Lusk, the new superintendent of Glacier National Park, turned his attention to improving facilities and enhancing the public's Glacier experience.

Gil Lusk, assigned superintendent of Glacier National Park in 1986, was a strong advocate of public use of Glacier. He argued, "The park can't exist in a vacuum. If tourism succeeds, then I know Glacier will succeed." He did not see a conflict between his mandate to preserve the natural resources and the need to

Prominent signs, as well as pamphlets, a ranger station handout, and various park brochures, warn visitors that Glacier is bear country.
Courtesy Glacier National Park Archives.

serve the public. He launched a number of programs to enhance the public services. Visitor facilities and concessionaire services were improved. The communities outside the park were encouraged to plan for growth to accommodate the predicted increase in visitors to Glacier. More winter use of the park for snowshoeing and skiing was promoted; however, the ban on snowmobiles remained.

The park expanded its nature walks, interpretive talks, and trail rides, which had been popular since the 1920s. New interpretative signs on trails and along the Going-to-the-Sun Road offered the public tidbits about the geology and wildlife of the park.

The park also broadened its environmental awareness programs, adding two educational programs for schoolchildren: the National Environmental Education Development Program and the nationwide Environmental Study Areas Program. Both were designed to teach kids about the importance of wildlife and the value of wildernesses.

In 1983 a private nonprofit organization in Kalispell, Montana, called the Glacier Institute, was formed to provide wildlife and nature education programs. "Think of it as a summer camp for kids and grown-ups alike, for mind, body and spirit," wrote

A grizzly bear and a ranger cross paths on the Hidden Lake boardwalk.
Photo by Brian Kennedy.

Then-Vice President George H. Bush with Glacier National Park Superintendent Bob Haraden and Wyoming Senator Alan Simpson on Logan Pass during their 1983 visit to the park.
Photo by Brian Kennedy.

the *Missoulian*'s Michael Jamison in 2007 of the then twenty-four-year-old institute. Self-described as "learning gone wild," the Glacier Institute is located just inside the west entrance of the park, and it uses the millions of acres of wilderness in Glacier National Park and the Flathead National Forest as its classroom to bring science and the wonders of nature to visitors. Learning about wildlife, wildflowers, edible plants, backcountry medicine, the stars, and glacial recession has grown increasingly popular with visitors over the years.

Native America Speaks

In the 1970s and 1980s there was a nationwide surge in interest in Native American tribes, who in turn sought to share their heritage with the public. The history of the region's tribes had long been chronicled inaccurately in Western novels and films and entwined with Old West legend. Their real history and culture was not widely known or understood.

In 1985 the *Glacier Natural History Association* began sponsoring a series of campfire programs known as Native America Speaks. The series was organized by Blackfeet troubadour Jack Gladstone, who wanted to share Blackfeet history and culture with visitors to the park. Over the years the program

Early 1900s Blackfeet horsemen look out over Cracker Lake.
Courtesy Glacier National Park Archives.

Blackfeet historian Curly Bear Wagner offers visitors a glimpse into Blackfeet history and traditions. Wagner, along with Kenneth Eagle Speaker and Darrell Kipp, who specializes in language, join Gladstone in bringing the Blackfeet culture to the public.
Ken West, 1993.
Courtesy Glacier National Park.

Jack Gladstone is the son of legendary Blackfeet storyteller Wallace Gladstone, the grandson of William Gladstone, who helped build Montana's Fort Benton and Alberta's Fort Whoop-Up, and the great-great-grandson of Blood Indian Chief Red Crow. Jack blends Blackfeet stories, legends, and history into song and presents them to guests at Glacier National Park.
Ken West, 1993.
Courtesy Glacier National Park.

has grown to include the history and cultures of the Salish and Kootenai tribes, who also played a part in the history of the land that now encompasses Glacier National Park.

In 1992 a special program titled Rediscovering America was presented to park visitors to coincide with the quincentennial of Christopher Columbus' landing in North America. Jack Gladstone's program reflected on some of the major cultural contributions of Native Americans to modern American culture. He honored three Indians whose talent and vision inspired their people and left a legacy for all Americans: Chief Seattle, the great orator of the Suquamish; Chief Joseph, who outwitted and outmaneuvered U.S. soldiers for 1,700 miles across Oregon, Washington, Idaho, Wyoming, and Montana in a failed attempt to lead 800 Nez Perce to Canada in 1877; and Sac and Fox tribe member Jim Thorpe, the 1912 Olympic gold medal winner in the pentathlon and decathlon, who was recognized by the Associated Press in 1950 as the greatest athlete of the first half of the twentieth century and the third-greatest athlete in history.

The Native America Speaks program has been recognized for "excellence in the interpretation of American Indian culture" by the Council for American Indian Interpretation and has expanded over the years to include drumming and dancing, as well as an environmental and heritage education program called Work House, which

was developed with an advisory group of Blackfeet, Salish, and Kootenai advisors and teachers. Native American exhibits have also become more prominent in and around Glacier, and there are plans to increase the Native American cultural presence in the park.

Iceberg Lake.
Photo by Tony Bynum.

14

Understanding a Changing World
1990–1999

T HE LAST DECADE *of the twentieth century saw the collapse of the Soviet Union, the official end of the Cold War, and the eruption of war in the Middle East. Economic recession hit, Western movies made a comeback, and health, wealth, and high-tech toys were on the most-wanted list. Natural disasters and global climate change took center stage in the 1990s. Hurricane Andrew pummeled Florida in 1992. The following year ten times the normal rainfall fell in the Midwest.*

The Mississippi River rose to its highest recorded level, flooding nearly fourteen million acres, forcing 100,000 people from their homes, and causing forty-one deaths. A 1994 earthquake rocked Los Angeles, killing sixty-seven people.

In Glacier National Park, science and research took on greater importance in park resource management. Ecologists studied the glaciers, which were melting at an alarming rate—and grabbing the attention of the White House. Biologists investigated the relationships between wildlife species and tried to figure out just how many grizzlies called the park home. Waterton–Glacier International Peace Park was designated a World Heritage Site.

Warming Warning
The phone rang at Dan Fagre's house, and his daughter Danielle answered. "Hello?"

"This is the White House calling," said the caller.

"Dad," she said, matter of factly, "it's the White House on the phone."

Fagre was the ecologist and global change research coordinator for the United States Geological Survey in Glacier National Park. As he picked up the phone, he wondered which of his colleagues was playing a practical joke.

It wasn't one of Fagre's buddies. It *was* the White House, and Vice President Al Gore wanted to set up a meeting. Gore chose Glacier National Park as one stop on his fact-finding mission focusing on global warming because of the park's renowned Global Change Research Program—and because Grinnell Glacier was quickly disappearing.

On September 2, 1997, the vice president flew into Great Falls, took a helicopter to Babb, and drove to the Many Glacier Hotel to deliver a speech.

Left to right, National Park Service ranger/ naturalist Dave Casteel, ecologist Dan Fagre, and Vice President Al Gore at Grinnell Glacier in 1997.
Courtesy Fagre Family.

Blackfeet Chief Earl Old Person, Glacier National Park's Superintendent Dave Mihalic, and Senator Max Baucus and Rep. Pat Williams of Montana attended the event, along with members of the public and national and local press.

Gore shared data gathered by scientists at Glacier's Global Change Research Program and from around the world, which revealed startling information: seventy percent of the ice that covered Glacier National Park in the last century was now gone, and ice all over the world was disappearing at an alarming rate.

After his speech, the vice president and an entourage of aides, secret service, park rangers, ecologists,

Vice President Al Gore with Glacier National Park ecologist Dan Fagre and family at Many Glacier in 1997. Left to right, Ann Fagre, Casey Fagre, Al Gore, Dan Fagre, and Danielle Fagre in front.
Courtesy Fagre Family.

*Grinnell Glacier
circa 1910.*
Courtesy Montana Historical Society,
Helena, Montana.

*Grinnell Glacier
in August 2000.*
©chuckhaney.com.

Logan Pass.
Courtesy Glacier National Park Archives.

Waterton–Glacier World Heritage Site logo. The Waterton–Glacier International Peace Park was inscribed as a World Heritage Site in 1995 and dedicated as such in 1998. The area encompasses one of the most ecologically intact areas remaining in the temperate regions of the world.
Courtesy Glacier National Park Archives.

and scientists, as well as Senator Baucus, Representative Williams, and Superintendent Mihalic hiked to Grinnell Glacier. Dan Fagre and veteran NPS ranger/naturalist Dave Casteel pointed out that just two days before Gore's arrival, a two-acre slab of Grinnell Glacier had broken off and become an ice floe on upper Grinnell Lake. Then they led Gore into an ice tunnel below the glacier to show the vice president how the glacier had both thinned and receded.

Studies indicate that the glaciers of Glacier National Park are excellent barometers of prolonged climate change. In 1850 there were more than 150 glaciers within the park boundaries. The larger glaciers are now approximately one–third the size they were in 1850. Numerous smaller glaciers have disappeared. Correlation studies between glacial retreat and local climate indicate that at the present rate of warming, all of the glaciers in the park will disappear by 2030. Even with no additional warm-

ing, the glaciers are likely to disappear by 2100.

A Treasure to the World

In 1932 Waterton Lakes National Park was combined with Glacier National Park to form the world's first International Peace Park, and in 1979 the pair was designated as the first Trans-Boundary Biosphere Reserve. Glacier had previously been designated a biosphere reserve in 1976. In 1998 the Waterton–Glacier International Peace Park was further honored with dedication as a World Heritage Site.

The United Nations Educational, Scientific, and Cultural Organization selects World Heritage Sites, recognizing these unique places as vital pieces of the "heritage of humanity." The World Heritage List includes more than 850 locations around the globe. Each country pledges to protect the cultural and natural resources of its heritage sites so that they may be passed on to future generations.

The creamy white flowers of beargrass and an elegant waterfall grace a hillside near the Garden Wall.
Photo by John Reddy.

In this case, the end of the rainbow is Glacier's Bowman Lake, located in the park's

15

Glacier in the Twenty-First Century 2000 and Beyond

E ACH DECADE SEEMS TO HAVE *had its ups and downs, and the first decade of the twenty-first century was no different. Americans were staggered by the terrorist attacks of September 11, 2001, war in the Middle East, and a variety of natural disasters— and rallied by giant leaps in science and technology that promised people could live longer, communicate electronically like never before, and explore the universe. The warnings of global climate change in the 1990s continued to be a hot topic in the twenty-first century.*

Glacier National Park experienced record snowfall, avalanches, floods, and forest fires. The Going-to-the-Sun Road underwent its most extensive renovation since it was completed in 1934. Global warming trends continued to melt the park's glaciers, foretelling their disappearance and forcing officials to take a hard look at the future of Glacier National Park in the twenty-first century.

The Fires of 2003

In 2000 the worst fire season in more than fifty years blackened 6 million acres nationwide and nearly one and a half million acres in Montana. Glacier emerged relatively unscathed that year with only several small lightning-ignited fires.

But 2003 was a different story. On a hot July day, fire lookout Travis Rosenkoetter spotted a fire from the Huckleberry Mountain Lookout. As Rosenkoetter was reporting the fire, he happened to glance at a letter he had been writing to his father, so he named the blaze the Robert Fire, after his dad.

The fire was started at what appeared to be a party around a campfire in the Canyon Creek drainage west of Glacier National Park. The fast-moving fire raced east from Canyon Creek, jumped the North Fork of the Flathead River, then roared up the southern toe of the Apgar Mountains toward West Glacier and Lake McDonald. Apgar and West Glacier residents watched in amazement as flames exploded on the ridge above the towns.

Firefighters hurriedly ignited a backfire to draft the wildfire to the north, away from Apgar and West Glacier. It worked at first—then the fire turned back, again threatening the towns. Residents, concession operators, and visitors were evacuated while firefighters lit blazes to eat up fuel and drive the fire away from

Apgar Mountain after the fire.
National Park Service.

Aerial view of the Robert Fire.
Somer Treat, National Park Service.

A burnout is started near Apgar and West Glacier to control the advance of the Robert Fire.
Courtesy Glacier National Park.

homes. Airplanes dumped thousands of gallons of water between the fire and the towns to create a wet buffer.

The fires caused the closure of much of the west side of the park from July 24 to August 4 and from August 10 to August 15, when Apgar and West Glacier were again evacuated. More than 900 firefighters battled the blaze, and eventually the Robert Fire was brought under control.

Lightning-ignited fires in the Trapper Creek area threatened Granite Park Chalet and burned on both sides of the Going-to-the-Sun Road until the flames were finally squelched in early September.

In all, forest fires burned 145,000 acres in Glacier National Park and another 165,000 acres just outside the park in 2003.

West Glacier residents watch as the 2003 Robert Fire blows up.
Somer Treat, National Park Service.

A helicopter drops a bucket-load of water on a controlled burn used to stop the advancement of the Robert Fire.
David Restivo, National Park Service.

A CanadaAir CL-215 firefighting plane lands on Lake McDonald.
Jean Tabbert, National Park Service.

On July 23, the Trapper Fire jumped the Going-to-the-Sun Road and burned the area known as The Loop.
National Park Service.

The Trapper Fire, viewed from Logan Pass.
David Restivo, National Park Service.

Water pours over the side of the washed-out slopes east of Gunsight Pass Trailhead between Siyeh Bend and Sunrift Gorge on the east side of the Continental Divide.
National Park Service.

A portion of the Going-to-the-Sun Road was washed out in 2006.
National Park Service.

Landslides washed out the Going-to-the-Sun Road and its earth-retaining slopes, as well as took out the culvert east of the eastside tunnel.
National Park Service.

Nature on a Rampage

When it came to natural disasters in Glacier, 2006 reigned supreme: avalanches, fires, and floods—and a state record wind gust of 164 miles per hour was recorded on Marias Pass.

Avalanche!

In January 2006 abnormally warm temperatures dropped unseasonable rain on the Continental Divide snowpack. The rains, like heavy snowfall, added additional weight to the snowpack; as rainwater seeped down through the snow, it loosened the layers of snow. Gigantic slabs of snow began breaking loose and tumbling down the mountains, uprooting

trees and bringing timber, rocks, and even animals with them. An avalanche slab below the Triple Arches plummeted down the slope, tossing trees into Logan Creek that later pulverized McDonald Horse Bridge and battered the Going-to-the-Sun Road.

Fire!

On July 28, six months after the avalanches were a melted memory, an employee at the St. Mary Visitor Center spotted a smoke plume near Red Eagle Lake. By the end of that day, the fire had consumed 250 acres. By mid-August it had burned 32,230 acres. More than half of the burn was in Glacier National Park. It engulfed nearly fifteen miles of trail, two footbridges, and two backcountry campgrounds at opposite ends of Red Eagle Lake. Nearly 200 firefighters fought to suppress the lightning-caused fire, which was finally contained in September.

Flood!

As if the winter avalanches and summer fires hadn't been enough, a warm wind—aptly named the Pineapple Express—swept through Glacier in November. Spawned by an El Niño eruption of warm water in the Pacific Ocean, the storm brought warm temperatures and heavy rain. Nine inches of rain fell in three days, once again sweeping the snowpack off the mountains.

Mud and rocks washed down and covered parts of the Going-to-the-Sun Road. Trees that avalanches had torn from the mountainside and deposited in Logan Creek eleven months earlier rushed wildly downstream, ramming the Going-to-the-Sun Road and prying up the pavement. McDonald Creek roared

Floodwaters cover the Going-to-the-Sun Road east of Avalanche Creek picnic area.
National Park Service.

McDonald Creek smashes the horse bridge on upper McDonald Creek and batters the McDonald Creek Overlook.
National Park Service.

Swollen Swiftcurrent Lake floods the Many Glacier Hotel and flows over the road in November 2006.
National Park Service.

Excavators remove stones and debris from the old rock guard wall in preparation for building new walls.
Shaun Bessinger,
National Park Service.

Hard-working, dedicated road crews remove the flood debris and repair the damaged Going-to-the-Sun Road in time for the opening on July 1, 2007.
Shaun Bessinger,
National Park Service.

and raged, smashing the horse bridge on upper McDonald Creek and battering the North Lake McDonald Bridge's foundation. Water gushed down Piegan Mountain. Between the East Side Tunnel and Siyeh Bend, 108 feet of roadbed collapsed and slid into the St. Mary Valley and parts of both lanes were washed out in five other locations east of Logan Pass.

In the Swiftcurrent Valley, Swiftcurrent Lake rose seven feet in twenty-four hours, finally peaking at nine feet. It flooded the basement of the Many Glacier Hotel. Eighteen inches of water flowed through the St. Moritz and Lucerne rooms.

Undaunted by the beating the park took in the winter of 2006, park employees and contractors converged the next spring to make emergency repairs to the Going-to-the-Sun Road in time to open for the 2007 season and clean up and repair the damage to the Many Glacier Hotel.

Nearly 200 dump trucks of debris were removed from where mudslides had dumped 1,500 to 2,000 cubic yards of mud, rocks, trees, and branches on the highway near the Loop and cleared another 1,000 cubic yards of debris that had buried the road near the Triple Arches and Haystack Creek.

The most monumental tasks were repairing the road east of Logan Pass, where the floods had torn out parts of both lanes in six locations. Among the re-

pairs to these locations were constructing a 350-foot mechanically stabilized earthen retaining wall, paving the roadway across the wall, and installing a 125-foot temporary bridge.

The floods of November 2006 caused at least $7 million in damage to the Going-to-the-Sun Road.

Going-to-the-Sun Road Showing Its Age

By the turn of the twenty-first century, the Going-to-the-Sun Road had been carrying visitors through the heart of Glacier National Park for nearly seventy years. The annual freezing and thawing in Glacier's harsh environment and the wear from millions of automobiles had taken their toll on the grand old road. Glacier's highway to the sky was showing its age and needed major rehabilitation.

In 2000 Congress passed a bill authorizing the Department of the Interior to fund studies on the road's

Visitors traveling the Going-to-the-Sun Road pass through the east-side tunnel, completed in 1931.
Photo by John Reddy.

A motorist drives past the Garden Wall along the Going-to-the-Sun Road, with Mount Reynolds in the background.
©chuckhaney.com.

rehabilitation. A number of studies culminated in 2003 for an eight- to ten-year plan commencing in 2006.

Rehabilitating the fifty-mile historic road requires bolting the rock cliffs above the Going-to-the-Sun Road to stabilize the sheer cliff face above Crystal Point and above the Loop, as well as bolting the rock formations in the Eastside and Westside tunnels. Various bridges will be rehabilitated, along with making improvements in culverts and cross and horizontal drains. Fourteen retaining walls will be either rehabilitated or completely reconstructed. Some of the historic masonry guardwalls will be dismantled and rebuilt.

Just as in the 1920s and 1930s, native stone will be used, some of which was salvaged from existing damaged walls. Mortar materials necessary to bond walls are similar to the historic materials.

The plan also calls for improvements to visitor facilities, including improved vehicle parking and pedestrian circulation at existing pullouts; construction of five new turnouts for slow-moving vehicles; construction of a few new short roadside trails and rehabilitation of the older trails; designation of transit stops at popular locations along the road; and improved interpretive information for visitors.

The cost to rehabilitate the road and improve visi-

tor use facilities is estimated to range between $140 million and $170 million.

Part of the plan to reduce traffic while the road is being rehabilitated is to provide a shuttle service, which began in 2007. The shuttle service differs from the red bus tours in that the shuttle is free, no interpretation is provided, and it stops at all major trailheads. Hikers can hop off one shuttle, hike point-to-point, and catch another shuttle back.

On the west side of the park, shuttle service begins one mile past the west entrance at the T-intersection near Apgar, where the Apgar Transit Center sits nestled in the trees. The transit center is the first new facility built in the park since the Mission 66 buildings of the 1950s and 1960s.

Wildlife

Glacier National Park abounds with wildlife. Nearly every species that Lewis and Clark documented while in the Northwest is still in Glacier, with the notable exception of bison.

The early twenty-first century has seen many advancements in our understanding of the unique creatures that call the northern Rocky Mountains home.

The Way It Was

When Glacier became a national park in 1910, rangers practiced "predator control," the practice of exterminating predators such as wolves, mountain lions, and coyotes, to encourage the survival of animals popular with tourists, such as bighorn sheep, goats, elk, and deer.

"Monsters" in the West

In the eighteenth and nineteenth centuries, in the East and in Europe it was widely believed that monsters dwelled in the West. The reports of gargantuan beasts and strange creatures were based on the stories of Spanish soldiers and French travelers and the sketches imaginative artists created after hearing their tales.

One of the many tasks President Thomas Jefferson required of explorers Meriwether Lewis and William Clark on their journey was to make observations and collect the skins of the wildlife species they saw. Jefferson particularly wanted information on animals that were native only to the West. Lewis and Clark found that many of the animals, such as the coyote, red fox, muskrat, and beaver, existed both in the East and West. The grizzly bear and the mountain goat were western animals no Easterner had seen. Lewis once had to dive into a river to escape a grizzly and noted in his journal that he "had reather fight two Indians than one bear."

At the turn of the twentieth century, hunting, trapping, and westward expansion brought the bison and the wolf to the brink of extinction, and grizzly bears vanished from most states.

Ground squirrel.
Photo by Randy Smith,
Missoula, Montana.

Bighorn sheep.
Photo by Tony Bynum.

Predator control ended in 1934 after the release of the "Fauna 1 Report." The report presented the case that predator control was adversely affecting the wildlife population at large and was throwing the web of life out of balance. In 1964 ecologist Starker Leopold and a group of scientists and wildlife experts authored a report to assist the National Park Service manage its wildlife. Known as the Leopold Report, it reaffirmed the Fauna 1 ideas of the 1930s and defined the goals of wildlife management as being "to represent a vignette of primitive America," which was interpreted as restoring the natural conditions of the park and wildlife to the time that explorers Lewis and Clark first ventured westward in the early nineteenth century. The report also strongly recommended using science and research as the basis for wildlife management. Various programs have since been launched by the National Park Services to enact the goals set forth in the Leopold Report.

Mountain goat.
Photo by Tony Bynum.

Watchable Wildlife

Biologists and wildlife experts spend long days in the field gathering information; they spend even more time analyzing the data. They study everything from the impacts of climate change on wildlife to the nesting habits and locations of loons and harlequin ducks. Over the years they have observed an abundance of interesting wildlife behavior.

One of the most mysterious and fierce animals in

Pika.
Photo by Randy Smith,
Missoula, Montana.

Young moose.
Photo by Randy Smith,
Missoula, Montana.

Glacier is the wolverine, a cousin of the weasel. Little is known about this animal, which looks like a small bear with short legs, but Glacier National Park biologists and the USFS Rocky Mountain Research Station in Missoula are trying to find out more. The study is only the fourth conducted on wolverines in the lower 48 states and the first ever conducted in Glacier.

Wolverines are known to range over a 300-square-mile territory, which is larger than that of grizzly bears. And even with those short legs, wolverines are able to move remarkably fast. In 2003 biologists Jeff Copeland, Rick Yates, and Len Ruggiero reported tracking, by satellite, a wolverine that climbed Mount Cleveland, moving 5,000 vertical feet in ninety minutes. The biologists have also noted that despite the roaming ways and fierce reputations of male wolverines they appear to participate in raising the kits.

Dr. Kim Keating of the Northern Rocky Mountain Science Center learned that while bighorn sheep cross the Going-to-the-Sun Road, their travels are

Wolverine.
Photo by Tim Rubbert.

Drake ringneck duck.
Photo by Randy Smith,
Missoula, Montana

DNA studies indicate there were 332 grizzlies in Glacier National Park in 2000.
Photo by Tony Bynum.

limited by St. Mary Lake and the Jackson and Black-foot glaciers, and consequently there are two genetically different sheep populations less than twenty-five miles apart.

Hair of the Bear

In 1998 Katherine Kendall, a U.S. Geological Survey researcher, and 200 field crew members began their ground-breaking study to use DNA from bear hair to determine how many grizzlies lived in Glacier National Park and the northern third of the Northern Continental Divide Ecosystem. She was able to identify species and gender and distinguish individual bears by examining DNA extracted from bear hair and scat. Wire "snags" were wrapped around trees that bears were known to rub up against, and "snag stations" were placed along bear travel routes and favorite foraging areas. Researchers simply checked the stations for hair, retrieved samples, and returned to the lab. Previously, bear populations were determined exclusively by sightings; however, because many bears look very similar, the accuracy of the data was questionable. In 2000 Kendall released her preliminary study, which showed there were 332 grizzly bears in Glacier National Park and 437 grizzlies in the northern third of the Northern Continental Divide Ecosystem.

The Howl of the Wolves

In 1985 a three-year-old white "alpha" female wolf and her seven pups came south with the first pack of wolves known to have entered Glacier National Park since the 1930s. This pack became known as the Magic Pack for their tendency to appear and disappear from researchers' watchful gaze. The white alpha female had been collared in Canada in 1985, and in 1986 she denned in Glacier—she is responsible for the first documented den in the western United States in more than fifty years. She raised five pups that year. In 1985 the Magic Pack split up, and she moved north

Grizzly bear.
Photo by Tony Bynum.

In 1993 both wolves and mountains lions were living in the area of the North Fork of the Flathead River of Glacier National Park, a circumstance that had not occurred for 100 years in the lower forty-eight states.
Photo by Donald M. Jones.

Lynx.
Photo by Tony Bynum.

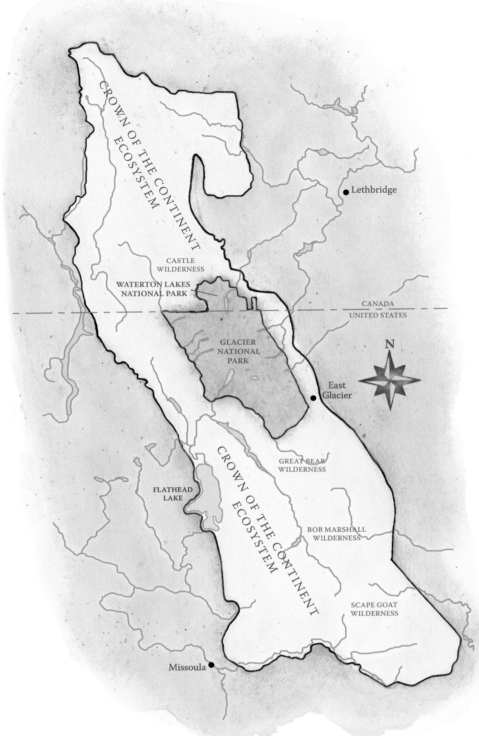

into Canada and raised another litter of five pups. Her radio collar failed in 1988, and researchers were unable to closely monitor her movements after that. She was occasionally seen in Glacier over the next two years, and she is then believed to have traveled to the Pincher Creek area in Canada. She remained there until she was killed by a hunter in 1993.

That same year there were three packs in Glacier, and most are believed to have been her direct descendents. In 2007 at least five packs were living in Glacier. Some, no doubt, are descendents of the white wolf of the Magic Pack.

Corridors to Survival

Glacier National Park plays a major role in the survival of North American wildlife species. Bears, wolves, cougars, and lynx travel long distances to find mates and denning sites, expand their territories, and migrate seasonally with the food supply. Migrating unobstructed between vast areas of wilderness by way of "wildlife corridors" is essential to many species' survival.

Glacier National Park, Waterton Lakes National Park, and the Bob Marshall Wilderness Complex comprise the Crown of the Continent Ecosystem, the core wildlife habitat of one of the premier mountain eco-regions of the world. It is a critical connecting link in a chain of vital ecosystems and wildlife corridors that extends from Yellowstone National Park in Wyoming to the Yukon in Canada.

Mountain lion.
Courtesy Glacier National Park Archives.

Glacier, along with various agencies and interest groups, is working to protect existing wildlife corridors against the onslaught of development and increased human populations in the northern Rocky Mountains.

Map of the Crown of the Continent Ecosystem

A grizzly bear spots a herd of unsuspecting bighorn sheep.
Photo by Tony Bynum.

The Future of Glacier National Park

In Glacier National Park's 100 years, it has grown beyond just a premier tourist destination; it has been recognized as an International Peace Park, a Trans-Boundary Biosphere Reserve, a World Heritage Site, and a global climate change research laboratory. Part of the Crown of the Continent Ecosystem, the park has been noted as one of the most ecologically intact areas remaining in the temperate regions of the world.

Despite a noble legacy, Glacier's future is threatened by outside forces such as growing population centers, mineral development, and global climate change.

Outside Threats

Glacier's future as a national park and as an intact ecosystem lies in the scientific studies of human impact on the landscape and wildlife.

Between 1990 and 2004, there was a 35 percent increase in population in Glacier and Flathead counties. As the resulting development spreads into forested areas, it disrupts wildlife movement and compromises water resources and air quality, to name only a few of the impacts.

In addition to the development pressures from larger populations near its borders, Glacier is facing the prospect of extensive mineral development across the border in the Canadian Flathead region, located in southeastern British Columbia and extending nearly forty miles along the North Fork of the Flathead

River, which forms Glacier's western boundary. The Canadian Flathead is a vital piece of the Crown of the Continent Ecosystem. It has unsurpassed water and air quality and provides important habitat for the grizzly bear and other wildlife species.

In 2006 the National Park Service issued policy to "use all available tools to protect park resources and values from unacceptable impacts" and to "encourage compatible adjacent land uses." This new policy expanded the responsibilities of park managers from the already weighty tasks of simultaneously maintaining the park's pristine wilderness and providing an enjoyable experience for visitors to include the broader role of working with government officials in the entire region to protect the resources of the Crown of the Continent Ecosystem and Glacier National Park.

Citizens and private organizations have joined park managers in the fight to protect Glacier's legacy and future.

Global Climate Change

Lurking on the horizon is another issue: global climate change. Scientists predict that at the present rate of melting, all of the park's glaciers will be gone by 2030.

This fact presents intriguing challenges to park officials. Do we still call the park Glacier National Park when all the glaciers are gone? Yes, of course, but

Reynolds Creek, Logan Pass.
Photo by Tony Bynum.

Wild Goose Island.
Photo by Tony Bynum.

greater issues abound. Prolonged warming or cooling creates a chain of ecological events. Vegetation responds to climate changes, and wildlife responds to vegetation changes. What will happen to the alpine species that thrive in the higher, colder elevations? What happens if bears don't hibernate? Will there be enough berries, bugs, and fish to keep them alive year-round or should the park supplement their feeding, and if it does, what effect does that have on bear–human encounters? The list of potential "ifs" is endless, and Glacier's scientists and park rangers are currently studying such scenarios. Many yet unknown challenges may also lie ahead in preserving this cherished landscape and its cultural resources for future generations.

Happy 100th!

Glacier National Park is a wonderland of awesome mountains and glorious valleys carved by glaciers thousands of years ago. It is a sanctuary for wildlife that once roamed the vast plains and mountains of the American West. It is a sacred place for the Kootenai (K'tunaxa) and Blackfeet (Piikáni) tribes, and its trails have felt the moccasined footsteps of the Salish, Nez Perce, Pend d'Oreille, Siksiká, Kainaa, Háninin, Tsuu T'ina, Absaroke, Cree, Assiniboine, and Shoshone tribes, as well as the hiking boots of nineteenth-, twentieth-, and twenty-first-century explorers and adventurers from around the world.

Glacier's wilderness survived the arrival of fur traders, miners, and railroad barons and found itself protected as a national park. One hundred years as a national park brought Swiss-style hotels and chalets, the Going-to-the-Sun Road, and millions of visitors from around the globe.

Deserving its designation as an International Peace Park, Trans-Boundary Biosphere Reserve, World Heritage Site, and global research laboratory, Glacier National Park is a magnificent, unparalleled work of nature. In this changing world, what lies ahead for Glacier National Park is partly in

GLACIER
NATIONAL PARK
1910 CENTENNIAL 2010
CELEBRATE. INSPIRE. ENGAGE.

Glacier Time Trek

A Chronology of Events

20,000 to 11,000 Years Ago

Ice age glaciers fill the valleys nearly to the tops of the mountains. As the earth warmed, the glaciers slowly moved downward, whittling the mountain peaks, scouring the valleys, and forming the landscape of Glacier and Waterton Lakes national parks.

8,000 to 10,000 Years Ago

Native Americans occupy the valleys and mountains of present-day Glacier and Waterton.

1500s & 1600s

1535 - French Navigator Jacques Cartier launches the fur trade near what is now Montreal, Canada. In 1668 Britain's Hudson's Bay Company is established and begins trading in furs.

1700s

1725 - The Niitsitapi (now known as the Blackfoot Confederacy) acquires rifles from the Cree and Assiniboine.

1732 - The Niitsitapi acquire horses for the first time.

- A smallpox epidemic kills fifty to eighty percent of the Niitsitapi (Blackfeet) population.

1763 - The British Army defeats the French. French possessions in North America are turned over to the British.

1792 - Hudson's Bay Company sends surveyor Peter Fidler to map the area east of the Rocky Mountains. Fidler gives first English place name of Kings Mountain to what is now known as Chief Mountain.

1800s

1803 - United States purchases the Louisiana Territory from France. It includes the area west of the Mississippi to the Rocky Mountains.

1803–1806 - Captains Meriwether Lewis and William Clark and the Corps of Discovery explore the lands of the Louisiana Purchase.

1805 - Lewis and Clark come close to what is now Glacier National Park but turn and pass to the south. Lewis names the Maria's (now Marias) River in honor of his cousin, Maria Wood.

1818 - Treaty of 1818 between England and the United States establishes the U.S./Canada boundary along the forty-ninth parallel from Lake Superior to the east face of the Rocky Mountains.

1823 - Trapper Hugh Monroe is sent by the Hudson Bay Company to live with the Piikáni tribe of the Niitsitapi. Later his life becomes legend in books by author James Willard Schultz.

1831 - American Fur Company trader James Kipp builds Fort Piegan at the mouth of Marias River to trade with the Piikáni (now known as the Blackfeet).

1840 - Robert Greenhow's report of the Northwest Coast of North America is published. Detailed maps were published in 1945.

1846 - U.S. and Great Britain agree on the forty-ninth parallel as the international border between the U.S. and Canada from the Rocky Mountains west to the Pacific Ocean. The boundary placed the land west of the Continental Divide in what is now Glacier National Park in U.S. territory.

1851 - Fort Laramie Treaty defines the Blackfeet territory as the Canadian border to the north, the Musselshell River to the east and south, and the Continental Divide to the west.

1855 - Hellgate Treaty is signed on July 16, 1855. The Bitterroot Salish (Flathead), Pend d'Oreille (Upper Kalispel), and the Kootenai (K'tunaxa) tribes form the Confederated Salish and Kootenai and agree to live on a reservation in Montana's Mission Valley.

- Lame Bull Treaty is signed on October 17, 1855 (also known as the Blackfeet Peace Treaty and the Judith River Treaty). Tribal territories were mapped. The Blackfoot Confederacy agreed that certain lands assigned them by the 1851 Fort Laramie Treaty would be shared for 99 years as common hunting ground. The Missouri headwaters region was to be shared with the western tribes, and lands east of the Milk River were to be shared with the Assiniboine. No lands were ceded to the U.S.

1864 - Congress creates territory of Montana.

1869 - John J. Healy and Alfred B. Hamilton establish Fort Whoop-Up and Joe Kipp establishes Fort Standoff, both in Canada. Whiskey trade flourishes.

1870 - Lt. Col. E. M. Baker leads the Second U.S. Regiment

the same night draws nationwide public attention, inspires a book, and changes bear management policies.

1968 - Glacier adopts the Starker Leopold Report's recommendation to restore Glacier flora and fauna "to represent a vignette of primitive America."

1970 - U.S. Congress passes National Environmental Policy Act. National Park Service increases focus on preserving ecosystems.

1971 - Glacier adds a backcountry ranger district and establishes new wildlife and wilderness management policies.

- Boardwalk to Hidden Lake at Logan Pass is started.

- Park officials encourage development of campgrounds outside of the park to meet increasing visitor demands.

1973 - U.S. Congress passes the Endangered Species Act.

1976 - Glacier National Park designated a biosphere reserve by UNESCO. Waterton is designated in 1979.

1982 - Waterton–Glacier International Peace Park celebrates fifty years.

1983 - Going-to-the-Sun Road celebrates fiftieth birthday.

- Going-to-the-Sun Road is listed on the National Register of Historic Places.

1985 - Going-to-the-Sun Road is designated a National Historic Civil Engineering Landmark by the American Society of Civil Engineers.

- The first wolf to den in the western United States since the 1930s moves into Glacier from Canada.

1987 - First annual Waterton–Glacier Peace and Friendship Days celebration.

1988 - The Red Bench Fire on the western edge of Glacier burns 27,500 acres in the park.

- A number of National Register–listed homesteads are consumed.

1990 - Waterton–Glacier International Peace Park designated to conduct global climate change research as part of the U.S. Global Change Research Program established by the U.S. Congress.

1992 - Committee on Improving the Science and Technology of the National Parks stresses science in managing the resources of the national parks.

1995 - Glacier celebrates eighty-five years as a national park.

1997 - Going-to-the-Sun Road is designated a National Historic Landmark.

1998 - Dedication of Waterton–Glacier International Peace Park as a World Heritage Site. (Parks were inscribed as World Heritage Sites in 1995.)

- First of two bear DNA studies, nicknamed "Hair of the Bear," to determine species, distribution, and population of bears in Glacier and surrounding areas begins.

1999 - National Park Service launches its Natural Resource Challenge Plan.

- Park releases its General Management Plan to guide management of the park for the next fifteen to twenty years. Plan honors public's desire to "keep Glacier as it is."

- Glacier's 1930s vintage red buses are removed from service due to safety concerns.

2000 and Beyond

2000 - U.S. Congress passes bill authorizing studies on Going-to-the-Sun Road rehabilitation.

- Preliminary results from "Hair of the Bear" DNA studies show there are an estimated 437 grizzlies in the northern portion of the Northern Continental Divide Ecosystem and an estimated 332 grizzlies in Glacier National Park.

2001 - Following terrorist attacks of 9/11, Glacier National Park invites visitors for an "open house" for unity, hope, and healing on Veteran's Day weekend.

2002 - Refurbished historic red bus fleet returns to Glacier and is placed into service.

2003 - The Robert, Wedge Canyon, Rampage, Trapper, Wolf Gun, and Middle Fork fires burn nearly 138,000 acres. The National Register–listed Cattle Queen Snowshoe Cabin burns. The 39,400-acre Robert fire threatens Apgar and West Glacier.

- Going-to-the-Sun Rehabilitation Plan Record of Decision signed November 5. The $140- to $170-million rehabilitation begins in 2006 and is expected to take eight to ten years.

2005 - The melting of glaciers in the park captures worldwide attention. Based on warming trends and impact modeling, the park's glaciers are predicted to disappear by 2030.

2006 - January avalanches uproot trees and jam creeks with debris; November floods roar through Glacier, destroying trails, roads, and bridges and damaging the Going-to-the-Sun Road.

2007 - Crews clean up the damage from the 2006 floods and begin repairing and rehabilitating the Going-to-the-Sun Road.

- The Apgar Transit Center, the first new visitor facility since the 1960s, opens.

- Waterton–Glacier International Peace Park celebrates seventy-fifth birthday.

2008 - Going-to-the-Sun Road celebrates seventy-fifth birthday.

2010 - Glacier celebrates 100 years as a national park.

2016 - National Park Service centennial.

Bibliography

Buckholtz, C. W. *Man in Glacier.* West Glacier, Montana: Glacier Natural History Association, 1976.

Campbell, Marius R. "Glacier National Park: A Popular Guide to its Geology and Scenery." Bulletin 600, Department of the Interior United States Geological Survey, 1914.

Chase, John. Various interviews and unpublished documents and displays. 2007.

Copeland, Jeff, Rick Yates, and Len Ruggiero. "Wolverine Population Assessment in Glacier National Park." U.S. Forest Service Rocky Mountain Research Station, 2003.

Diettert, Gerald A. *Grinnell's Glacier: George Bird Grinnell and Glacier National Park.* Missoula, Montana: Mountain Press Publishing Company, 1992.

Dyson, James L. "The Geologic Story of Glacier National Park." Glacier Natural History Association, Special Bulletin No. 3, 1949.

Fagre, Daniel B. "Adapting to the Reality of Climate Change at Glacier National Park, Montana, USA." U.S. Geological Survey proceedings paper, Conferencia Cambio Climático, Bogota, 2005.

Fagre, Daniel B. Various U.S. Geological Survey publications. Northern Rocky Mountain Science Center, 2006.

Fagre, Daniel B, Ann Fagre, Wendy Hill, Lon Johnson, Jack Potter, and Deirdre Shaw. Personal interviews and miscellaneous documents. Glacier National Park, 2007.

Hall, Myrna H. P., and Daniel B. Fagre. "Modeled Climate-Induced Glacier Change in Glacier National Park, 1850–2100." *BioScience,* Vol. 53, No. 2.

Hanna, Warren L. *Stars Over Montana: Men Who Made Glacier National Park History.* West Glacier, Montana: Glacier Natural History Association, 1988.

Jackson, John C. *The Piikani Blackfeet: A Culture under Siege.* Missoula, Montana: Mountain Press Publishing Company, 2000.

Lepley, John G. *Blackfoot Fur Trade on the Upper Missouri.* Fort Benton, Montana: River and Plains Society, 2004.

Loeffler, Don. Various unpublished documents. 2007.

Lomax, Becky. "Glacier's Wildlife Sleuths." *Montana Magazine,* May/June 2006.

Martin, Steven P. "Record of Decision for the Final Environmental Impact Statement for the Going-to-the-Sun Road Rehabilitation Plan." National Park Service Intermountain Region. November 5, 2003.

McClintock, Walter. *The Old North Trail: Life, Legends, and Religion of the Blackfeet Indians.* Lincoln, Nebraska: University of Nebraska Press, 1968.

Morrison, Chris. *Waterton–Glacier International Peace Park: Born of a Vision.* Waterton, Canada: Waterton Natural History Association, 2007.

Olsen, Jack. *Night of the Grizzlies.* New York: Putnam Publishing, 1969.

Parrett, Aaron. "Montana's Worst Natural Disaster." *The Montana Magazine of Western History,* Summer 2004.

Prato, Tony, and Dan Fagre. *National Parks and Protected Areas.* Ames, Iowa: Blackwell Publishing, 2005.

Reeves, Brian, and Sandra Peacock. *"Our Mountains are Our Pillows," an Ethnographic Overview of Glacier National Park.* West Glacier, Montana: Glacier National Park, 2001.

Reeves, Brian, Amanda Dow, Richard Hughes, Doug Mitchell, Margaret Newman, Kevin Thorson, Mack Shortt, and Dale Walde. *Mistakis, The Archeology of Waterton-Glacier International Peace Park. Archeological Inventory and Assessment Program 1993-1996 Final Technical Report.* Bozeman, Montana: Montana State University and the National Park Service. 2003.

Robinson, Donald H., and Maynard C. Bowers. *Through the Years in Glacier National Park.* West Glacier, Montana: Glacier Natural History Association, 1960.

Ruhle, George C. *Guide to Glacier National Park.* Minneapolis, Minnesota: J. W. Forney, 1949.

Sax, Joseph L. and Robert B. Keiter. "Glacier National Park and Its Neighbors: A Twenty-Year Assessment of Regional Resource Management." The George Wright Forum, volume 24.

Sellers, Richard West. *Preserving Nature in the National Parks.* New Haven, Connecticut: Yale University Press, 1997.

Index

Page numbers in italic indicate images

R

Ragged Woman, *72*

Randels, "Dad," 48

Reagan, Ronald, 30, 101, 102

Reed, Roland, 11, 14

Reeves, Brian, 10

Reiss, Winold, 71–72, *72*

Reno, Marcus, 31

Repeat (bear), *64*

Reuter, Jack, 43

Reynolds, Albert "Death on the Trail," *43,* 48, *50,* 50–51, 85

Reynolds, Mount, *vii, 141*

Reynolds Creek, *146*

Rinehart, Mary Roberts, 32, 45

ringneck duck, *143*

Rising Head, 21

Rising Wolf, 21

Rising Wolf, 65

Robert Fire, 135–36, *136, 137*

Rockwell, Mount, *58*

Rogers, Will, 45

Roosevelt, Franklin Delano, 58, *58,* 83, *84,* 95

Roosevelt, Theodore, 43, 45

Rosenkoetter, Travis, 135

Rudberg, Charles, 76

Ruder, Mel, 100

Ruggiero, Len, 143

Ruhle, George C., 77–79, *78,* 99, *105*

Running Crane, *42*

Russell, Charles M., 10, 16, 28, 45, *45*

Russell, Nancy, *45*

S

Salish, 88, *89*

Schultz, James Willard, 21, 29, 31, 32, *33,* 33–34, 45

Seyler, Julius, 71

Shepard, Lou, *80*

Sheridan, General, 26

Shoshone, 7, 11, 147

Siksiká (Blackfoot), 7–8, 12, 13, 18, 19, 20, 29, 147

Simpson, Alan, *126*

Sinopah Mountain, *58*

Sioux, 7, 12

Snyder, George, 37, 56, 64–65, 66

Snyder Hotel, 56

Snyder House, 64

Solomon, Mose, *29*

Somes, M.P., 77

South Piikáni, 9, 12, 13, 26

Speaker, Kenneth Eagle, 127

Speed, Clarence, *51*

Sperry, Lyman B., 32, 45, 50

Sperry Chalets, 51, 57, 59, *59*

St. Mary, *109*

St. Mary, 66

St. Mary Bridge, *68*

St. Mary Chalets, 51, 57, *57,* 83, 98

St. Mary Falls, *120*

St. Mary Lake, *66*

Stanwyck, Barbara, 30, 101, *102*

Stevens, Isaac, 12, 15, *24,* 24–25

Stevens, John F., 25, *25,* 35, 123

Stimson, Henry L., 30

Sully, Alfred, 26

Swanberg, Steward, 96

Swanson, Bill, 65–66, 67

Swanson, William, 51

Swiftcurrent Auto Camp, *96*

Swiftcurrent Lake, viii, *93, 139*

T

Taft, William Howard, 47

Tail Feathers Coming-over-the-Hill, 33, *42*

Thacker, Blaine, 124

Thomas, Charles, 28–29

Thompson, David, 18

Thompson, Jim, *121*

Thorpe, Jim, 127

Three Monarchs, xi

Three Suns, *42*

Thunder, 10

Tinkham, A.W., 24, 25

Trail Makers, The, 11

Trapper Fire, *137*

Triple Arches, *74, 76*

Tsuu T'ina (Sarci), 8, 147

Two Medicine Chalets, 51, 57, *57,* 58, *58, 84*

Two Medicine Lake, *58, 65*

U

Upper K'tunaxa, 13

Upper Pend d'Oreille, 15

V

Van Allen, C. F., 43

Van Orsdale, John T., 44

Vaught, Henry, 48

Vaught, L. O., 45

Vint, Thomas, 74

W

Wagner, Curly Bear, *127*

Walter, Dave, 96

Water Hole, The, 14

Waterton-Glacier International Peace Park, *85,* 85–86, *86,* 88, 123, 124, 129, *132*

Waterton Lakes National Park, 10, 13, 14, 17, 18, 51, 55, 85, 120, 124, 132, 145

West Glacier Bridge, *110*

Wheeler, Burton K., 89

Whilt, Jim, 61, *61*

Whitcraft, Tom, 50

White, Walter, 67–69

White Calf, 41, 42, *42*

White Grass, *42*

White Head Calf, 10

Wilderness Act, 115, 119

Wild Goose Island, *147*

Williams, Pat, 130, 132

Wirth, Conrad, 102

Wise, Robert L., 69

wolf, *119, 144*

wolverine, *143*

World War II, 85, 95–98, 107

Wynn, Mount, *84*

Y

Yates, Rick, 143